Christmas 09.

Hope u cike this
Book Thomas
Happy Reading

BREAKFAST THE NIGHT BEFORE

From: Mum xxx

Breakfast
the Night Before

RECOLLECTIONS OF AN IRISH HORSE DEALER

Marjorie Quarton

THE LILLIPUT PRESS

DUBLIN

First published 2000 by
THE LILLIPUT PRESS LTD
62–63 Sitric Road, Arbour Hill,
Dublin 7, Ireland
www.lilliputpress.ie

A CIP record for this title is available from
The British Library.

3 5 7 9 10 8 6 4 2

ISBN 1 901866 56 4

*The Lilliput Press receives financial assistance
from An Chomhairle Ealaíon / The Arts Council of Ireland.*

Set in 11 on 15 Sabon
Printed in Ireland by ColourBooks of Baldoyle, Dublin

CONTENTS

PREFACE

When *Breakfast the Night Before* originally appeared in 1988, the publishers, André Deutsch, were in the process of changing hands and not running as smoothly as before. As a result, although briefly a bestseller, the book was reprinted only once and has been in demand ever since. It never appeared in paperback, and has been unobtainable for years. I followed it up with another memoir, *Saturday's Child* (1993), very few copies of which reached Ireland. The present book consists of parts of both of these, and much more. I have omitted much that is no longer relevant, brought the events up to date, and added a lot of new material.

My life has been unusual in many ways, and often amusing, so I have tried to entertain rather than inform. I have sketched in my background and my childhood, which was of the kind called 'privileged'. I have shown how I rejected the life mapped out for me and chose another, while remaining, of necessity, at home. I have tried, rather than mingle the various strands of my life, or lives, to take different aspects of each in turn, while gradually moving forward to the present day.

My whole life has been spent among animals; often they have taken the place of people – I have sometimes been lonely. As people live more and more in towns or suburbs, they realize less and less what it is like to be surrounded by livestock. A little boy was visiting my home some time ago and I showed him an egg, which a hen had laid under some bushes.

'A wild egg,' he said, astonished. 'Is it full?'

This is not an animal book as such. Horses, dogs and farm animals share it with people who cared for and cared about animals. You can care about a creature whose destiny is to be eaten. Don't ask me how or why. I am sure that looking after animals is good for you, therapeutic if you like. Even a hamster or a bowl of goldfish can make you feel good, so I'm told.

I am sometimes asked if it was hard to move from my cosy niche into the rough world of horse-dealing. Thinking back, I'm sure my biggest handicap was my upbringing. 'She's well brought up – that must count for something,' said my parents when I strayed from the appointed path. I was crippled by that gentle rearing. I was unable to be deliberately rude; to hurt feelings (even when they begged to be hurt); to stand up for myself. 'You'll get nowhere in this lark,' said a dealing friend, 'you have a heart like butter.' Again and again, I lost out financially because I'd been trained to think the best of everyone. Circumstances forced me to harden my butter heart, but I didn't really change.

Horses can be addictive, and so can dealing. When addicted to both, you can easily come to grief. I survived. The stories in this book are true, except perhaps for some told to me by others. The people are real, and I have changed names only when it seemed advisable.

MARJORIE QUARTON
October 2000

CHAPTER ONE

Starting Young

I can't remember a time when horses meant nothing to me. Born and reared on the working farm where I lived until recently, they were always there in the background when I was a child, part of my life. I used to get out of bed and sit on my window seat, listening to the carthorses in the stables, listing the different noises they made. Scrunching hay, scrunching mangolds (much louder), snuffling after mislaid grains of oats, snorting, stamping and rattling halter chains. Sometimes there would be a great, grunting sigh and a clatter as one of them lay down. They were called Andy, Dandy and Fred.

The stables were out of bounds when the horses were in. They were tied up in a row with their heels towards the door, and I had the rashness born of ignorance which is sometimes mistaken for courage. I was about four when it dawned on me that the worst that would happen to me was a not very hard slap if I were caught. Well worth the risk. I crept out to the stable and made several unsuccessful attempts to climb onto the back of the nearest horse via his manger. Fred took no notice. Then, just as I was about to give up, Andy, the biggest of the three, lay down. I climbed onto his wide, dusty back and sat there happily for ages. I suppose I was missed, for somebody came running out, my nurse probably, saw me and gave a piercing scream. At once, it seemed as if an earthquake had started. Andy rocked from side to side as he organized himself for getting up. He tipped back, paused and then seemed to shoot towards the roof. It is my first clear memory. My hands were so tightly twisted into his long, greasy mane that I couldn't have fallen off if I'd tried. My father had to be fetched to get me down, and there was no slap.

After that, Rody, the ploughman, used sometimes to lift me onto Andy's back. Rody, nicknamed 'the Robin', and his son Paddy, who inherited the nickname along with the job, worked here for more than half a century between them. Once, Rody put me up on Andy's bare back just before it was time to go to a children's party. I was wearing a pink frock with matching knickers and Andy had been working hard all day, carting manure. My mother was not amused.

Clearing out some old letters a few years ago, I found an essay I wrote when I was five. It was done in careful capitals and entitled MY PONY. I had written, MY PONY IS CALLED ANDY. HE IS 17 HANDS. I LOVE ANDY. HE IS DED.

Andy died of tetanus. I crouched on my window seat, watching as the vet came and went. The paraffin lamps lent extra drama to the scene and I shivered as I listened to Andy breathing. It was a frightening sound, like a giant in distress, and, suddenly, the breathing stopped … I have never forgotten that night, and never will.

I transferred my affection to Fred, who was, like Andy, a bay Clydesdale. He had a long, sorrowful white face and a perpetually drooping lower lip. I used to slip into his stall and feed him cabbage leaves, toffees, and bread and jam.

Over the stable was a musty, cobwebbed hayloft whose floor was highly unsafe. The rotten boards were patched with biscuit-tin lids. There was a ladder up to the loft, simply asking to be climbed. When it was pointed out to me that toffee might be bad for Fred's teeth, I climbed into the loft and pushed quantities of hay down to him instead. My enthusiasm was such that I posted myself down along with the last armful and nose-dived into the manger after it. Fred seemed only mildly surprised.

Fred was named after Fred Minnitt, the friend my father had bought him from. Rody always called the horse 'Mr Minnitt', thinking, I suppose, that 'Fred' would be lacking in respect.

I may have suggested that I had a good deal of freedom when I was small. Not at all. My life, up to the age of nine or so, was so sheltered it was a wonder I didn't suffocate. Most of my early memories are of walks with my nanny, securely held by the hand, bonneted and gaitered in the manner of the time.

I loved Greta, my nanny, dearly, and wouldn't have dreamed of revealing that she pared her corns with my father's cut-throat razor. Because of those corns, our walks weren't the brisk affairs they were meant to be; most ended a few hundred yards up the road in some cosy cottage, where Nanny drank stewed tea and talked to her friends about deaths and diseases.

I think I was fairly well behaved, so few scoldings and fewer slaps came my way. An only child, I shared my parents' affection with various cats and dogs but with no other child. Kept at home, I saw no other children. Nanny took me for walks while my parents walked the dogs, but I saw nothing to resent in this arrangement. My mother wondered if I was jealous of her cat when I dropped him out of an upstairs window – and this is the only occasion I can remember when she was really angry with me. In fact, I'd been told that cats always landed on their feet and was checking. It is true. However, my mother had seen Cromwell, so called because he was remarkably ugly, falling past the drawing-room window, and I failed to convince her.

*

When Nanny had her day off, my mother didn't exactly take over, although I think she sometimes took me out in my pram. She was nervous of me, not being of the generation which bathes and changes its babies. My father was nineteen years older and in poor health. I can't imagine his reactions if he could hear about the domestic duties of the 'new man'.

I was usually left in the care of the cook or the housemaid and they competed to spoil me. The spoiling flagged when I didn't want to go to bed and the poor girls wanted to go out and meet their boyfriends. Because of this, I was taught that, once in bed, it was wise to stay there for fear of bogey men. As well, I learned always to keep my hands under the sheets. This was to discourage thumb-sucking, I believe. I was told that the child who was foolhardy enough to leave so much as a finger out of bed might have it taken and shaken by an ice cold hand, while a menacing voice asked, 'How are you keeping, this fine night, Miss Marjorie?' It was years before I outgrew my fear of the phantom hand.

Sometimes, the maids tired of minding me, and let me run out to the yard and 'help' Danny or Edmund with the milking, or feeding the calves. As I lived in total isolation from other children, I didn't miss their company and was perfectly happy most of the time. My parents were thirty-two and fifty when I was born, and I grew from a toddler to a little girl with a distinctly middle-aged view of life. I was four years old when I first saw a baby. I'd been told of the treat in store and imagined something like the toothlessly smiling infant sitting on a cushion on the tins of Allen & Hanbury's rusks. I couldn't wait. Nanny took me to our neighbour's house, where the mother was busying herself in the kitchen with a basin, towels and soap. I looked around eagerly but saw no sign of a baby. A towel was spread on the table, and on it a small purplish red creature lay on its back, eyes screwed shut, fists in the air. My innocent question, 'What is it? Is it cooked?' earned me a stinging slap and a scolding. My yells woke the baby, who added his own, and I realized my hideous mistake.

Even then, I hardly believed I was looking at a human infant; one moreover who was called Francis Joseph and is now a retired schoolmaster. I wasn't easily forgiven.

*

I went to hardly any parties. As for birthdays and Christmas, they were times for presents but not for outings. The presents were of three kinds: books, chocolates and money. The chocolates were hidden and doled out at a rate of two a day. The books were hidden too, until my mother had read them to make sure they were 'suitable'. The money disappeared into the Post Office. I became adept at finding the chocolates and the books, which I read in the airing cupboard. But the Post Office beat me; it seemed an unfair place to hide presents as they never re-emerged. I hadn't grasped the principles of saving and wouldn't have been impressed by them if I had.

My chance to beat the system came when I was nine years old. My grandmother gave me two pounds for my birthday – actually put two green pound notes in my hand. 'Get your mother to put it in the Post Office for you,' she said.

My mother was going to Nenagh to have her hair done and took me with her. By then, the nannies had long gone and she often took me with her – not that she ever went very far herself. I was clutching my £2, so soon to disappear for ever. The hair-dresser was a patient lady called Miss Ryan, who needed all her patience when I exchanged Nanny for a governess who made me learn a hymn by heart every Sunday. When my mother took me with her, I sang these hymns to Miss Ryan, and my mother, deafened by the roaring dryer, didn't know what was happening. As soon as she could get a word in, Miss Ryan would give me twopence and tell me to run up to Gleeson's Fruit Shop and get an ice-cream.

On this momentous birthday, my mother went to a different salon, Hassey's, in Barrack Street, where sales of pigs and calves took place. I wandered out and watched. The calves were in carts, drawn up on either side of the street, with the horses facing outwards. There were also pigs, whose deafening squeals filled the air as they were prodded and pulled about.

I walked along the row of carts, looking into each one, the money crumpled in my hand. A stout man in a raincoat asked, 'Buy a calf, Miss?'

Buy a calf? Why not? With the Post Office waiting to swallow my money, it seemed a good idea. 'How much is the roan one?' I asked. The man asked £4, I craftily offered ten shillings. After spirited bargaining, in which at least a dozen bystanders joined, I bought it for £2 and the man spat on a threepenny bit and gave it to me for luck. I asked him to deliver the calf to my home, a distance of more than four miles. He agreed, reluctantly, urged on by my supporters. I think he was expecting to have to return the money and take the calf back. Instead, when he reached my home, he persuaded my father to buy the other calf, a white one which died almost at once.

I named my calf Polly, after my grandmother, but this was said to be cheeky, and her full name, Caroline, only slightly less so. I thought of the horse, Mr Minnitt, but I could hardly call my calf Mrs Smithwick, and Granny sounded wrong for a week-old heifer. I called her Starr in the end, after the man who sold her to me. Some time afterwards, my father sold Starr for £3 and put the money in the Post Office for me. This started in me a lifelong distrust of almost all financial institutions.

*

Although I became a horse dealer when I was still in my teens, when I was younger, horses were the only stock I never dreamed of selling. Our carthorses worked until they died or were pensioned off or put down. I loved them all and would have been deeply shocked if one of them had been sold. Cattle were a different matter and I was fascinated by the fairs which were held in the streets on the first Monday of every month. The noise, dirt and general chaos were profoundly appealing to a child kept in a nursery and bound by an unchanging routine.

The calf, pig and fowl markets were quieter and more civilized affairs, except at Christmas. Pig dealers, who could easily be recognized by their bowler hats and the way they wore their socks outside their trouser-bottoms, were considered to be farther down the social ladder than cattle or sheep dealers. At the Christmas market, pork pigs and kid goats were sold, as well as every kind of poultry.

Geese were more popular than turkeys in the country, and there was a great trade for them. They used to be sold wholesale to dealers who shipped them to Liverpool, then marched them across England in droves to Manchester, Leeds, York and even Newcastle. Geese are great walkers – fortunately – but their feet wouldn't stand up to so much roadwork. Accordingly, at the port, they were driven first through soft tar, then through sand. After this treatment, they were as good as shod. No wonder Irish geese were more renowned for muscle than fat.

We never bought anything in the market except my calf. The turkey market was an uproarious affair, and got more so as the day progressed. Farmers' wives had few opportunities to go to town, and for many, the turkeys were their only income. Fierce bargaining took place, and acrimonious arguments. I remember a grey-haired woman, tall, broad and determined, who wore a black hat rammed down on her head, a man's black frieze coat and nailed boots. She could out-shout any man in the market and outswear him too. She started a violent argument with a usually peaceable butcher, about the weight of a tremendous old cock turkey. The bird, feet tied, was clutched in her powerful arms, and its face and hers were alike red and furious. Bets were laid and a crowd gathered outside the butcher's stall. The butcher lost his nerve and refused to weigh the turkey on the spring balance in his shop. Next door was a chemist's shop with a wicker-basket scales for weighing babies. The woman charged into the shop and dumped the bird in the basket, where it turned the scales at forty pounds. She then marched out in triumph to collect her winnings, without a word to the scandalized chemist.

My parents avoided fairs and markets unless they had business there; neither could understand my fascination with them. I didn't either, but I had a feeling of being in my real element. I wanted to buy and sell, and the noisy crowds didn't bother me at all. I was a born dealer and it was lucky that, when I was young, I had no money to lose. I'm still dealing.

CHAPTER TWO

Family Glimpses

Elderly people are often accused of seeing the past through rose-tinted spectacles. I'm sure the reason for this is that my generation and the ones before were out of touch with reality. Unless you were starving, fighting in the trenches or doing social work, your vision was blinkered by lack of communication and by censorship. Television and the press now bring every aspect of crime, misery and vice to our sitting-rooms. No wonder that, as we grow older, the past seems rosier, the present gloomier.

The sun in those bygone days shone all through the summer (but not enough for the crops to fail), young people joyfully obeyed their elders, women were beautiful, men were brave and handsome, marriages were happy. Horses were plentiful and cheap; foxes were plentiful too, and ran tirelessly across the grass fields in the winter sunshine. There was no barbed wire hidden in the (neatly clipped) hedges, and the teller of the tale, if he is to be believed, was always well to the fore. He was never afraid, never fell off and his horse never went lame.

Most of this of course is untrue. I think we did have less rain. The spring which supplies my house with drinking water hasn't run dry for many years but, when I was a child, we used to fetch water from Lough Derg every day in summer, in barrels. Yes, we drank the lake water. We boiled it but we drank it. Who would drink it now unless strained and pasteurized? We weren't fussy. We knew that cattle stood flank-deep in the lake, keeping cool. Honest dirt, we said, never hurt anyone.

As for young people obeying their parents, I think they did. I accepted that my father's word was law and seldom questioned my mother. It was many years before I started trying to escape from the way of life which had been chosen for me. Other young people were coerced into jobs they hated because of family tradition. This could lead to a whole lifetime of frustration and regret.

An extreme example at an earlier date was that of my father's family. His father was a clergyman, so there was no land to be allocated. The eldest son was told to join the army, the second (my father) was earmarked for the navy, the third would (of course) enter the Church. No plans had been made for number four, who was much younger.

Uncle Charlie was killed in South Africa at seventeen by a Zulu spear and his body never recovered. My father, happily preparing to join the navy, was rerouted into the army. He was upset. He argued. But he went. A good rugby player, he told me that one of his worst moments ever was when he had been capped to play for Ireland, but sailed for South Africa instead, on the day of the match. Uncle Fritz was studying Divinity and was grudgingly allowed to continue and little Uncle Algy was steered early into the navy. He must have done all right as he got to be an admiral, but he said he only joined to please his mother.

His mother was granny – Granzie as the family called her – and few people argued with her. I remember her as an alarming old lady, tall, straight and bossy. 'You'll turn out just like your grandmother,' was my mother's worst threat. She may have had a point ... Granzie, friend of Maud Gonne, Mrs Sheehy-Skeffington and other movers and shakers, chained herself to the railings in College Green and hurled women's suffrage pamphlets over the balcony in the Gaiety. She loathed Bernard Shaw and had an incandescent correspondence with him, so I have been told. If only the letters had survived!

As Granzie told me how meek and obedient the children of her day had been, I wondered in my muddled way how this generation of slaves had grown into fearless, independent adults, such as Granzie herself. She was keen to go to prison to help the Suffragettes, but being the widow of the Chancellor of St Patrick's, failed to realize her ambition. She championed all kinds of lost causes and was an ardent Nationalist and Republican. When she died, it turned out that she had lent money to many people, and been a loyal friend. She certainly never obeyed anyone.

*

Granzie's mother was the last person born and reared at Bunratty Castle before the family abandoned it and built what is now the Bunratty House Hotel. I belong to the Smithwick family who first came to Ireland about six hundred years ago and have remained ever since. I dislike being classified as Anglo-Irish, but there seems to be no escape.

My Smithwick forbears originally settled in Wexford and Kilkenny, where some of them founded the noted brewery. John Smithwick, of the so-called 'Protestant branch', lived at Athassel Abbey House, near Golden in County Tipperary. Two hundred years ago, he had a lot of land, a lot of money and a son who inherited a tidy fortune. This John had six sons and built houses for all of them. One, Garrykennedy, was to be a three-storied affair, but the money ran out halfway up the stairs. They clapped a roof on, and all the gracious bedrooms have sloping ceilings. The largest house was Shanbally House Stud; the smallest was Crannagh, where I lived for much of my life.

The sons died young, or produced only daughters, as was so often the case in such families. Two generations later, I, the only child of the head of the family, was having a hard struggle to keep my home and land. Only a strong physique and a dislike of being beaten enabled me to do so.

My mother was born and grew up in England, but had many relations in Ireland: Russells, Coghills and Somervilles. She lived in Ireland for fifty years, but had never wanted to. She didn't unpack her trunks for several years. She returned to England after I married – but only for two months. It had changed; she was glad to get back. We shared a home until she died and, twenty-one years later, I often miss her. She was such good company and the most loyal person I have ever known.

My father inherited Crannagh from his great uncle Robert, to his own delight and my mother's horror. They moved here in 1929. (Fifty years to the day later, my mother died.) When they arrived, the place was run down to a degree. Uncle Robert was blind for many years before he died, and his daughter and son-in-law weren't good farmers or even capable land-owners. My parents inherited, along with the farm, four men and four woman employees. As the house had been empty for several months and an inefficient cousin was 'running' the farm, it was somewhat over-staffed and under-financed.

The cook and housemaid were still there when I was old enough to ask questions and they told me some odd things. One was that Crannagh had been used as a 'safe house' by Michael Collins more than once during the Civil War, although this was strictly De Valera country. Another was that the family car, taken by raiders, was the original 'Johnson's Motor Car' of a popular song of the time. Great Aunt Emmy, the last of the family to live at Crannagh before my parents, was adept at the art of burying her head in the sand, and not one word of these things ever reached my parents except what I learned and told them myself. 'I don't think we want to hear about that sort of thing,' said my mother and her friends.

CHAPTER THREE

Horse Mad

When the Second World War broke out, Ireland was just recovering from a different kind of conflict – the Economic War. This was more of a deadlock than a war and, like most wars, was hardest on those who least deserved to suffer.

When De Valera came to power, he was intent on a self-sufficient rural community. He refused to pay the required annuities to England, and the British government retaliated by imposing heavy tariffs on Irish produce. Ireland then raised her own tariffs, and the result was a crash in prices, the wholesale slaughter of calves and the ruin of farmers who depended on the cattle trade for their living.

De Valera had wanted to transfer the cattle-dealers' power, which was considerable, to tillage farmers, as tillage provided more employment than stock. Employment would cut down emigration, and small-holders would be able to survive. This was the general idea, but it didn't work. Looking back over old account books, I read of bullocks bought at £14 each being sold a year later for £6. Calves were worth the price of their skins. We were lucky, having my father's British army pension, which paid the wages and the housekeeping; others sold out to the Land Commission, becoming in effect tenants of the government. Young people emigrated in droves.

I can't remember too much about it, being a small child at the time when things were worst, but a few memories remain. My father bought a small red and white heifer from an elderly widow, who had come to the house with a hard-luck story. He had been refusing to buy from half the countryside as he was believed (wrongly) to be wealthy. The farm was already overstocked, the bank manager getting peevish. When the woman, who was evidently desperate, explained that the heifer was all she had to keep her until harvest, my father gave her £5 for it, which was double its market value. Even so, she would have had no more than 10 shillings a week to live on until her acre of oats was fit to sell.

The heifer was very tame and I used later to ride on her back. We called her 'the Widow's Mite'. Unknown either to the widow or to us, the Mite was in calf, and produced a black heifer calf. So we kept her for a cow and a very bad one she was.

The worst of the Economic War had passed by 1934, but farming remained bad right up to the start of the Second World War, and cattle prices never really recovered until the seventies. I can remember the drovers who walked their cattle all day and slept at the side of the road at night, travelling from fair to fair. Some dealers could afford 'hackney cars' or taxis, but many walked their own beasts, about eight or ten miles a day in all weathers, selling as they went. In summer they put grass in their boots to keep their feet cool; on wet fair days they stood in the rain until the water ran out of their boots. Many of the drovers were ex-servicemen from the First World War, unable to survive on their pensions.

Constant wettings led to arthritis, rheumatism and TB. On the other hand, people on the whole grumbled less, and they certainly had fewer heart attacks.

*

Although I spent a lot of time with farm animals, I wasn't encouraged to ride when I was small. I never owned what could be termed a child's pony – not when I was small enough to ride one. Having started riding on Clydesdales, nearer seventeen hands than sixteen, I thought a pony a terrible comedown. Riding the carthorses bareback was something of a balancing feat, but otherwise easy. They responded to commands like sheepdogs. 'Hup off' or 'Come in' would turn them left or right. 'Hup' was for forwards, 'Way' for backwards and 'Sight' (or would it be 'Site'?) for stop. I gave these orders in a loud gruff voice, and it took me years to break myself of saying 'Sight' to my hunter when I wanted it to stop.

Perhaps if a quiet pony had been provided for me, I would have been less determined to climb onto the back of any four-legged animal that would allow it. My father had inherited Andy and Dandy along with the farm. I was happy enough clumping around on their broad backs until I saw the foxhounds in full cry. Then I began to dream of speed and thrills and to beg for a pony. For years, I begged in vain.

I have a snapshot of myself on Fred, wearing a tidy jacket and a pair of pint-size jodhpurs, made by Mr Condon the tailor. (I remember sitting on his counter, drawing faces on somebody's cut-out suit in tailor's chalk.) My feet are in the stirrup leathers, because my legs are too short to reach the irons. I am profoundly happy. Then my mother shouts from an upstairs window, 'Get that child a hat!' She, of course, is picturing me being dragged by one of those stiff, curling stirrup leathers and probably killed; she means a hard hat.

I slide off Fred (it's like sliding down a roof), run indoors and clap a hat on my head. To me at five years old, a hat is a hat. The one I am wearing in the snapshot is a broad-brimmed affair in yellow straw with a wreath of buttercups and satin bows.

When Fred died, I tried riding Packy, a black horse with a nasty temper from having been backed under heavy loads. He used to turn his head and snap at my toes with long, discoloured teeth. I begged and begged for a pony.

When I acquired Martin, a smart little roan, I thought he would be easier to ride than the carthorses because he was smaller. I was wrong. He was difficult to catch and, once caught, difficult to ride. Martin was only 13.2 hands, but he was a cob rather than a pony. He was a thickset roan with a mind of his own. The idea was that he would be useful on the farm when I had outgrown my passion for riding. He certainly did his best to cure me, usually by stopping dead and dropping his head. I would slide bumpily, head first down his bristly hogged mane, and Martin would tip me over his ears and trot away. I fell off him every time I rode him – sometimes several times – and he didn't respond to any of my commands. In fact he was boss. I cried for hours when he was sold. I wonder why.

I was about eight when Martin was sold and I decided to ride something safer, namely either the Widow's Mite or a red cow called Adelaide. I rode them in from the field at milking time, and both were far better schooled than Martin – although that wasn't saying much.

I suppose I had a way with animals, because I had little trouble in taming and training the cattle. I never tried saddling one, but as soon as I was tall enough to get onto their backs I took to riding the bullocks round the fields. I made string halters for them and gave them names. One of my favourites was called Blue Peter after the Derby winner of that year.

My parents decided that such dedication deserved a better mount, and bought me an elderly black pony called Pippin. She had a hollow back which made a nice change. Cattle are not designed by nature for bareback riding. Pippin was more like a little hunter. I taught her tricks and played all sorts of games with her.

One of these needed my father's help. I was the Flower of the French Cavalry or a Death's Head Hussar, according to which war we were fighting; he was unshaken infantry. He knelt on one knee, aiming a shooting stick, and Pippin and I charged him. Pippin would sheer off at the last second and I, more often than not, fell off. I enjoyed these simple war games enormously, and began to improve on them. I invented one in which I cut the heads off thistles with a sword (a real one) while galloping bareback across a field.

This activity was discovered and stopped, but not before I'd fallen off several more times, usually on my head. It was lucky for me that only the thistles were decapitated. After that, my father taught me to fall on my feet like a cat. I started my falling-off lessons in the haybarn, tumbling off the patient Pippin backwards, forwards and sideways. Then I graduated to jumping off at every speed up to a gallop. It was great fun and I'm sure that it's almost as important to learn how to fall off as how to stay on. In all the years I rode young horses, I never broke a bone, and my back injury was the result of a pitching headlong down a flight of marble stairs.

Because of these lessons, I wasn't frightened of falling, so I seldom fell. I always landed on my feet unless the horse came down too, when I tucked my head in and rolled away. Old hands tried to scare me with tales of crucifying falls; of the 'croppers', 'crowners', and 'vet and doctors' they'd survived – just. I remained unimpressed and confident until my young horse caught his foot in a hidden strand of wire on a narrow bank. That day, I rode home wearing the brim of my bowler hat round my neck, in a sort of happy stupor. I don't know why my head didn't hurt. About a mile from my gate, I began to have grave doubts about my direction. I'm glad to say that my horse knew his way home, so I was spared the humiliation of asking a neighbour.

*

To return to the time when I got Pippin, I quickly became that familiar thing, a horse-mad child. I felt that all time not spent with ponies or horses was wasted. I remember, but can't place, a verse I read years ago, which must have described the feelings of many parents, certainly my own:

> I love my child – I like the horse –
> But this is what is sad.
> The two together, night and day,
> Will drive me mad ...

Always a voracious reader, I turned from the Waverley novels, through which I had been doggedly worrying my way, and read only 'pony books'. This genre must have had its day – I don't see many of them in the shops now. Probably girls of from ten to fourteen years old mostly read adult books, comics or teenage romances. In the forties, pony books were everywhere and I had a cupboard full of them in my room.

These works had titles like *A Pony for Penelope, A Hunter for*

Henrietta, *A Cob for Kate*. They were never called *A Gelding for Gideon* or *A Filly for Philip*, because they weren't written for boys. The children were always female, about twelve years old and spoiled rotten. The ponies on the other hand were usually male, about 13.2 and only partly spoiled. Penelope or Kate sorted them out in time to win the bending race in the last chapter.

The books were always illustrated, often beautifully, so that the not so well informed could see just what a bending race was. It suggests a gymnastic competition to the non-horsey.

I used to think that some day I would write a pony book of my own (*A Mare for Marjorie*), and I made several attempts to start one. The problem was that the books were written to a formula outside my experience. They were generally set in the Home Counties of England, where kind Mummies and Daddies bought ponies for their children as a matter of course. The Daddies, although generous, were uninterested. They spent their working hours in London offices and their leisure playing golf. The Mummies, once horsey little girls themselves, were more helpful.

Although the story lines were simple, the language was not. 'Isn't he a teeny bit overbent, darling?' Mummy would enquire anxiously (all those bending races). Or 'Do be careful, Samantha, Topper's getting behind his bit.'

Where else could a pony be in relation to his bit except behind it? I wondered. Ahead of it? Surely not.

The books were always full of instructions about riding and stable management; sometimes sound, sometimes not. I learned a good deal. Some of the terms defeated me and it was no good asking my father, who despised the books heartily. I asked a friend to translate Samantha's request, 'Mummy, shall I give Topper a direct aid?' and Mummy's solemn reply, 'Very well, darling. Just this once.'

'A direct aid's a crack down the ribs with an ashplant,' said my foxhunting friend. I filed this information away, wondering why Samantha couldn't be more explicit.

How I envied those spoilt little girls with their yellow polo-necked jerseys, their velvet caps, jodhpurs and shining jodhpur boots. My own jodhpurs had been outgrown within weeks. I was growing like a willow and my riding dress consisted of boys' corduroy shorts, snake-buckle belt, bare legs and sandshoes. The top half of me was dressed in anything that came handy. My saddle was kept for special occasions, partly because it was unlikely to be replaced, partly because the leathers pinched my bare knees and the irons chafed my bare insteps. I rode much better without a saddle anyway.

As I grew older, I realized that I was luckier than Kate, Samantha and the rest of them, because they had to clean all their tack every day and were hedged around with rules and regulations. ('Darling! You can't go riding like that. You haven't oiled Pixie's hooves.') When my girth burst out hunting, I hung the saddle on a gate and continued happily without it until nightfall. When I got home, I couldn't remember which gate I'd left it on and there was trouble, so I got my bike and found it at last. Samantha would have had her pocket money stopped for that.

Of course by the time I was ten or eleven years old, my life had ceased to be sheltered. Europe was at war, the last of my governesses had gone and I was left to my own devices. My parents seldom made a fuss as long as I appeared at mealtimes. There was one time when I was in real trouble. I was obliged to wear a plate to straighten my teeth and it flew out of my mouth as I fell off into a deep ditch. I didn't see any reason to search for the hated object, but my parents did and I had to go back to the place every day and look for it. The search was abandoned after a week and my teeth stayed crooked.

The children in the pony books were easily pleased when it came to presents. Acceptable gifts included stable rubbers, neckstraps, curry-combs and curbchains. I distinctly remember a child being thrilled when Mummy presented her with a bucket and broom for mucking out.

The information in the pony books stopped short at breaking in. For this, I turned to Western movies. Nothing could have been further from the schooling received by my pony heroes. Breaking in, I believed, was done by lassoing a horse and allowing it to buck itself to a standstill. The cowboy would then bound on to its back, waving a ten-gallon hat and shouting, 'giddy-up' or some such encouragment. After this, the horse was said to be broken in. It could be bridled and, with a maximum of rearing and frothing at the mouth, controlled.

The first animal I tried to break in myself was a two-year-old pony filly which was being grazed on the farm for the summer. I was eleven years old and made up in recklessness what I lacked in sense. I lowered myself onto her back from the branch of a tree, having haltered but not bitted her. I think she was too astonished to buck, or perhaps she didn't know the rules for broncos.

I had been riding her for a week before I tried putting a bit in her mouth, and the only time she ever bucked was the first time she was saddled. My parents had no idea what I was up to until then. After that, my father explained about mouthing, long-reining and backing, and I broke in another pony.

Most of my tack was made up of odds and ends of trap harness. For reins, I used lampwick, a lovely soft substance which I haven't seen for years, ideal for the job. The rotten leather constantly broke, and was replaced with lengths of doubled twine or with wire. I was also adept at riveting the broken ends together.

*

In my late teens, I moved on to training horses both to saddle and harness for pay – if you could call it that. The going rate was £5 for about a month's work, and including necessary expenses such as shoeing. When I upped my price to £7, my customers complained bitterly.

Mostly, the horses were neither well-fed nor well-bred enough to give me much trouble, but I earned my money with the others. One of them, a ewe-necked grey, had his head set on at such a curious angle that it was impossible to mouth him properly. I clamped his head down with a standing martingale and took him out hunting. After a spectacular succession of rears and fly-jumps, he broke the martingale and ran away with me down a nearly vertical slope, dotted with gorse bushes. The slope lay between the Killaloe Road and the Castlelough graveyard. As my mount hurtled downwards, I felt we were heading for the right destination.

We rolled the last dozen yards and I escaped with nothing more serious than an earful of mud – literally. I had to go to the doctor to have the last of it removed.

Soon afterwards, this horse's owner took him to Limerick fair and sold him as 'regularly hunted by a lady'. I didn't hear of this description until after he had been sold to Tommy Grantham, who asked me if I was the lady in question. He also asked if I had got the grey ready for the fair. I then saw that his mane had been plaited in long pigtails, each finished off with a bow of blue hair-ribbon.

Samantha's Mummy would have been horrified.

CHAPTER FOUR

Dublin in Wartime and Desperate Remedies

Before I went to school in Dublin, I used to love going there. In fact the high spot of the year was being allowed to go with my father to directors' meetings of a firm which has since expensively collapsed. My mother preferred to stay at home, and it was fine with me, as my father got expenses for two and took me instead.

Dublin in wartime was a backward leap of fifty years, hard to imagine for anyone who doesn't remember it. The trains – steam of course – were fuelled by turf instead of coal and travelled fitfully from station to station, with occasional pauses in open country. Percy French described this sort of journey better than I can. The Nenagh-to-Dublin train took three hours to travel a hundred miles – officially. Sometimes it was more like six. It wasn't possible to get there and back in a day, or even two. We spent two nights away.

We used to go up by the afternoon train, arriving at Kingsbridge, now Heuston Station, in the dark. This was what I'd been waiting for. Rows of outside cars and four-wheeled cabs called 'growlers' stood on the platform where the trains drew in.

If I travelled with my mother (dentist, Christmas shopping), she chose a cab. They kept us warm and dry, even if they did smell of sweaty horses, stale stout and mice. They were mostly drawn by heavy draught horses which were a sorry lot. They were clipped out, but their big heads and bristly legs gave them away. Many were on their last legs, poor old things. Thinking of them brings back the memory of Stockholm tar and Jeyes' Fluid, sovereign remedies for almost anything.

I don't blame my mother for choosing a cab rather than a side-car. A visit to 'the City' meant best clothes: a hat, silk stockings, high heels. In cold weather, one gets colder and wetter in a sidecar than in any other vehicle except a gig. Car-men are said to be permanently deaf in their forward ear from the cold wind constantly blowing in. I believe it. My father, who didn't worry about his clothes or mine, could be persuaded to take a sidecar unless it was actually pouring. (Only tourists call the cars and car-men jaunting cars and jarveys.) The cars travelled twice as fast as the cabs and cost twice as much. Sometimes, on a quiet stretch along the quays, the car-man would let me drive – or rather, hold the reins, which were snatched back in a minute or two.

The car horses were well-groomed and their harness cared for. Many had bells on their collars, oiled hooves, ribbons in their manes. They stuck out their necks and tore along. I was as happy as could be, but my happiness was clouded when I discovered that they were often old or useless racehorses. They trotted in that slap-happy way because they had been 'denerved', a drastic cure for navicular disease.

One night, our car-man was drunk. He raced his horse after other drivers, shouting 'Hoi!' whenever he overtook one. He tore straight past our hotel and into St Stephen's Green, where he pulled up at the Shelbourne. 'We're staying at the Hibernian,' said my father, 'turn round.'

'You should stay here,' said the car-man, 'it's better.'

'Turn round.'

'I will not.'

'You'll get no fare if you don't.'

The car-man did a U-turn and took us back, cursing all the way.

There must have been hundreds of cabs and cars in Dublin. To see them turn out in strength, you had to be there on a race day. Phoenix Park, Leopardstown, Baldoyle – they even went out into the country to Fairyhouse and Punchestown. You could see an endless string of cabs going home at night, the horses wearily plodding along. There used to be a coach and four taking racegoers to the 'Park'. This was something of a gimmick, and it set off and returned at set times – no use to a serious punter and drinker. 'I like my transport to be elastic,' said one. When I went to school in 1945, the motor cars were still off the roads, up on blocks in the garages. The Dublin streets were just as they were in James Joyce's time, with only the electric trams and an occasional taxi among the horse-drawn traffic. The Post Office vans with their smart bays and Johnston Mooney & O'Brien's bread-vans outlasted most of the horse–drawn traffic. Last of all went the brewers' drays. The horses seemed to disappear overnight, and the taxis were back; great American cars, sprung like feather beds. It is sentimental to regret the passing of the horse traffic, when you remember how they worked until they were worn out, and even Stockholm tar and Jeyes' Fluid couldn't help them any more.

*

At home, the horses and cattle had a much better time, but our veterinary expertise left a lot to be desired. Outside, I got underfoot quite a lot and helped a little. I learned to milk, to separate the cream, to churn and make butter. I learned to teach calves to drink from a bucket by letting them suck my fingers in the milk, then taking the fingers away. I learned that calves had a habit of dying.

Looking back, I think we must have lost about one calf in four. Of course there were no antibiotics and the value of calves was small, but we tried valiantly to keep them alive. They were sewn into sacking jackets if they got pneumonia, and dosed with frightening mixtures. A 'green bottle', containing arsenic among other things, was a tonic; a 'black bottle' (treacle, liquorice, linseed oil) was a sovereign remedy for pneumonia; a 'brown bottle', containing ginger, honey and poteen, was a kill-or-cure medicine which seldom cured. Poteen on its own could almost raise the dead if not overdone – it is still sold as a medicine.

As I got bigger, I spent more and more time looking after sick or lame horses. Really looking after them. Sitting up at night, fomenting joints, poulticing, stouping, bathing … and, of course, preparing invalid diets for the sufferers.

In these enlightened days, it is unusual for a horse to need prolonged treatment if he is sick or lame. How did we manage without antibiotics? Badly.

A little boy at a show told me, when I admired his pony, 'Sometimes he gets sick. Then the vet comes and gives him the needle and he's okay again.'

'Do you know what the vet gives him?' I asked.

'He gives him the needle,' said the young horseman, impatiently. 'Like I told you.' It was easy to see that he thought me pretty dense. I was reminded of my veterinary cupboard with its jars, rusty tins, bandages and sinister little blue bottles marked POISON. This was where we kept the 'cures' I mentioned earlier: the treacle, the glucose and the blisters, red, green and black in order of severity. These were usually mixed by the vet, but we always kept some proprietary medicines as well.

One such, Reducine, was and I'm sure still is invaluable – for horses. It is a thick, tarry ointment, good for obstinate swellings and enlarged joints. I had a schoolfriend whose waistline was her despair. She wasn't a horsey girl, so she fell for the name – Reducine – Reducing! She asked me to give her some and I did – a jarful. I don't think I knew what she meant to do with it. I hope I didn't. She rubbed it into her midriff and, although she lost no inches, she was nearly driven mad by a horrendous crop of blisters. Moral? Take the label at its word when it says 'For veterinary use only.' Neatsfoot Oil will not give you a Mediterranean tan.

Some old-fashioned remedies can more than hold their own today. Friar's Balsam, the stuff our parents used to inhale from a kettle, with a blanket over their heads, was a great favourite. But its value is not only as an inhalant. Used as a rub, it takes the pain out of bruises and the swelling out of joints, human as well as equine. Another remedy with the same properties, Tincture of Arnica, disappeared for many years, but can now be bought from herbalists.

When nobody had heard of equine 'flu, and antibiotics were in their infancy, strangles was treated with hot fomentations and coughs with cough mixture. These were added to the food, but all kinds of remedies were forced down the throats of horses in need of a tonic. I knew a groom who used to make an 'electuary' out of honey and iron filings. He assured me that it worked, but warned that the iron filings must be free from rust.

Colic was a big bogey in the days when someone had to cycle five miles for the vet, who might be out anyway. Bread soda and warm water was good – if you could force it down the horse's throat as he thrashed about and tried to lie down. 'Let him lie down and sit on his head,' said some. 'Rub his flanks with turpentine and lead him about,' said others.

We were replacing our heavy carthorses with active Irish draughts, and by far the handsomest was a grey called Paul, by the local stallion, Jack Steel. Paul was subject to unpredictable fits of temper and also to attacks of colic. The vet was fetched to one of these; an excellent vet but elderly and not at all active. Paul was pawing the ground in a corner, blowing and showing the whites of his eyes. The vet studied Paul's expression closely, then he said, 'I feel it would be unwise to upset him further. I can tell he's feeling better – I should allow nature to take its course.' Afterwards, if he was called to attend to a horse, he would ask, 'Is it the grey?' If the answer was yes, an assistant would be sent.

We dosed horses with a long-necked bottle; the vets used a stomach tube, inserted up the horse's nostril. The medicine was then poured into a funnel. The uninitiated should never try this, as if the liquid goes into the patient's lungs instead of his stomach, he will drown.

Another thing sometimes forced down horses' throats, but only by the unscrupulous, was butter. A pound of butter was said to prevent the horse from whistling when he was galloped for his wind. I would have expected it to prevent him from galloping too, but apparently not.

Horses have a nasty habit of developing warts, especially the troublesome flat kind known as angleberries. If these are sited on a vein they can become cancerous; at best, they are unsightly and often placed where saddle or bridle will rub them. Old people charmed warts off animals and humans by impaling snails on thorns at the full moon or dropping straws down wells, with suitable incantations. The less superstitious used a lethal mixture of arsenic and hog's lard. If the patient licked it off, his worries were over along with his warts. He was a goner.

The dreaded farcy was also cured by a charm. There was a man who went about curing farcy with unfailing success. Unfortunately, there was a snag. Your horse would survive, but you would lose another animal within the month. Many risked it, hoping to lose a cat rather than a cow.

Talking of cats, the most desperate remedy I ever heard of is a cure for capped hocks. You kill a black cat (no, a tabby won't do), or if kind-hearted, wait until you find a black cat which has died a natural death. You cut it open and tie it round the horse's hock, fur side out By the time the cat has, so to speak, melted away, the hock won't be capped any more. Cat lovers could try using vinegar and sugar and lead instead, another frighteningly poisonous preparation.

When I was going to the Creamery every day, there was a farmer there whose cart was drawn by a horse which had got a bang on the eye, which had filmed over. The owner used to chew tobacco and spit the juice into the eye – which cleared, for whatever reason.

Hazel bark has known medicinal properties. Pond's Extract was made from it and was considered indispensable. I have also heard that repeated rubbing with a hazel switch will take away a curb. I don't think anyone believed this except the owner of the curby horse who rubbed away for weeks without effect.

Another easily obtained and cheap remedy is wet mud. As a face-pack it will beautify your skin; in its usual, less appetizing guise it is a cooling agent. There's nothing like standing for hours in a muddy gateway to cool tired joints if you are a horse.

Paul, he of the funny temper, suffered occasionally from kidney trouble as well as colic. We tried the excellent remedy of giving him a raw potato for his kidneys. For anyone who cares to try this – and it works – I must emphasize that it should be a large potato. Paul swallowed a little one whole and it jammed. It's a long way from a horse's front teeth to the narrow part of his gullet, where small objects stick. My father, knowing how easily a horse can choke, rolled up his sleeve and retrieved the potato. He assured me that Paul was a sensible horse and wouldn't dream of biting his arm off. Knowing Paul, I wouldn't have banked on it.

Pregnancy testing? Simple. No more hanging about behind a funny-tempered mare with a bucket, waiting for a urine specimen. Give the mare a drink of cold water while the Angelus is ringing on a saint's day. The foal, better informed than one would expect, is sure to kick. I tried this on my own mare, Matilda. I waited impatiently with my bucket of water and, at the first stroke of twelve on All Saints' Day, I offered it to her. Matilda wasn't thirsty. You can take a horse to water …

Stout used to be a popular tonic for horses before the price of a pint rocketed. We all know it put the sparkle in Arkle. Brewers' horses, fed on brewers' grains and sometimes slops, could become alcoholics and develop withdrawal symptoms when they changed hands.

Nobody is likely to lament the passing of treatments such as firing, when often the cure was worse than the disease. But I don't want to imply that the prod of a needle solves everything.

You never know when a black cat might come in handy.

CHAPTER FIVE

Down on the Farm

Both my parents were great believers in hard work to form character. I was expected to work rather than amuse myself when I was among the farm animals.

As I got bigger, I progressed to driving the carthorses. Paddy, the ploughman, was endlessly patient, so was Edmund, the herd. At Paddy's house, as a small child, I sat on his knee eating oranges and drinking goat's milk, or listened while he played the Harvest Time Jig on his melodeon. Of course, the time would come when these men would have to take orders from me, and I would have to try to keep their respect without losing their affection. I was lucky in managing to achieve this, and both stayed on until they retired.

By the time I was twelve, I could drive most horse-drawn implements. My father wouldn't have a tractor on the place, so, until he died, many years later, I worked horses in shafts and in chains, single and double. The heavy horses had been replaced by clean-limbed, active Irish draughts – an unwelcome change for the workmen who had grown used to a leisurely pace. I never tried ploughing because Paddy, very sensibly, wouldn't let me, and I only once drove three horses in the reaper and binder, but I tried everything else.

Driving the swath-turner in the hayfield was one of the most boring jobs on the farm, and one often allotted to me. I wanted to drive the tumbling rake, a flat affair which gathered the hay into piles. The driver would, when the rake was full, lift a wooden handle which made the rake somersault and deposit its load of hay for 'tramming', as it was called in my area. The word 'tram' for a haycock was a shortening of 'tramp-cock' as these large cocks of hay were trampled down as they were built, to make them firm. The tumbling rake was not an implement to daydream behind. If it was carelessly tumbled the tines could stick in the ground and impale the driver; if the horse stopped suddenly, the rake could turn over against his back end. I wasn't allowed to drive the tumbling rake until I was twelve.

Windrowing hay with the wheelrake was heavy work for a child, but it was one of my regular jobs for years. Paul was my favourite workhorse because he walked so fast in chains that I almost had to run to keep up with him. This was probably why there was so little competition to drive him. In the wheelrake, he strode along, his handsome head in the air, his ears pricked. It was like driving a good hunter.

Ecologists bewail the scarcity of corncrakes, skylarks, butterflies and various other birds and insects. So do I. But I do not regret the passing of the wild black bee. I expect some of them are still around – it is usually gentle creatures that become extinct – but they no longer nest on the ground in hayfields. As long as I live, I will never forget the day Paul put his hoof in a bees' nest.

I was turning the rake at the end of a swath and, as I was only just tall enough to press the lever which lifted the teeth of the rake, I was standing on it. This was mildly dangerous, like standing on the pedals of a too high bicycle, but necessary, as I needed both hands for the reins. Paul suddenly leaped forward, I fell back, grabbed the seat and just missed falling under the rake. At the same moment, two bees stung me, on the face and neck.

The seat of an old-fashioned wheelrake is high, hard and precarious. Its wheels are high too, and fastened to the axle with a single pin for easy removal. I clung to the seat with one hand, the reins with the other, my foot still on the lever. Bees whizzed past my ears as Paul raced across the field as fast as he could lay leg to the ground. Paddy and Edmund, who had been 'heading' the trams made the day before, began to run, shouting advice. Then, I think, they began to pray.

Paul kept going until a wheel came off the rake; then he swung round in a circle and stopped, as I tumbled on to the ground between his heels and the tines of the rake. Heaven knows why he stopped – if he hadn't, I wouldn't be writing this. I crawled out, my face swelling from the stings. I have been terrified of bees ever since.

A neighbour of mine, Jack Quinlan, had a similar accident with a wheelrake some years later, but his horse – a three-year-old – didn't stop and he was seriously hurt. I bought that three-year-old for £38 and she later became an international showjumper, changing hands for the then unheard of sum of £9000. Her name was Sugar Bush.

*

When I started breaking horses to harness, as soon as they were mouthed I would attach them to a 'clod-crusher'. This implement was a primitive device if ever there was one, being merely a slab of slate drawn by two chains. The idea was that there was little of value for the youngster to break, but it was slow work walking behind on the ploughed and harrowed ground. One could, of course, if suicidally inclined, ride on the clod-crusher as on a skateboard, and I sometimes did this.

When I think of those great rough creatures with their iron mouths and huge feet, and remember the crazy things I did with them, I realize that I must have led a charmed life.

The only major disaster I can recall took place in harvest time, when there was a rush on and, as well as a young horse, the gardener and the postman had been pressed into service. It was wartime, and we were obliged to till more land than we had horses or hands to work.

I was driving the young horse, a blocky little short-striding animal called Stumpy. I was riding on the first of two loads of wheat coming up the narrow, stony lane from the field to the farmyard. Stumpy slipped and fell, both shafts snapped and the entire load of corn landed on top of the horse with myself somewhere in the middle of it.

Paul, drawing the second cart, had no room to get by, and as he became frightened, the postman dared not leave his head. I couldn't move either, having been almost knocked out by a violent blow under the chin from the hames: we waited for someone to find us.

When eventually someone came, the load was forked off and Stumpy got up, his knees streaming with blood. I got into big trouble over that. But when I look at the place where it happened over fifty years ago, I wonder how horses ever pulled loads over those slippery rocks without falling. They must have led charmed lives too.

When I was about ten, my favourite task was driving the pony and trap – provided I was allowed to do so alone. Somebody had told me that if I drove the pony fast enough, he wouldn't have time to fall. There is a serious flaw in this reasoning, but he never did.

On Sundays, I decanted my parents at the church door and then drove the pony to Jerry's Yard, the livery stable, as fast as he could go. We tore straight down the main street and took the right-angled turn on one wheel. Having handed the pony over to Jimmy Reardon or his father Jack (I don't remember a Jerry) I ran all the way back, taking a short-cut through the Catholic church grounds and arriving at the Protestant establishment when the service was well under way.

At last, the rector's wife suggested that I should sit in the gallery at the back as I disturbed the worshippers when I charged panting up the aisle. That is how I joined the choir – musical ability had nothing to do with it.

*

In the war years, many people drove fast horses, and road races were popular. One in particular, the subject of astonishing wagers, took place after a funeral. The distance was seven miles, from Toomevara to Nenagh, and a grey thoroughbred mare was made favourite. In the end she was beaten by a half hackney. This horse, a black, used to trot with his head right up in the air and twisted to one side, while gobbets of froth from his mouth blew back and spattered his driver all over. Hackneys were not generally admired in Ireland. 'Lifting up his feet like a turkey in a stubble field,' said one scornful observer.

However, the black was unbeatable at trotting. Horse racing on the Dublin Road today is unimaginable.

These horses would trot at twelve or even fifteen miles an hour, but most driving animals achieved eight or less. Very slow and stately was Captain Finch's progress in an old brougham borrowed from my father. He had a cob to pull it, and had unearthed a coachman's livery, complete with cockaded hat. The coat was in tatters, but he managed to persuade his farm workman to wear it. When the weather was fine, instead of driving, Captain Finch rode the cob to church, accompanied by his terrier, well named Bouncer. The cob was tied up outside, and Bouncer sat in the pew where his violent scratching, the rattling of his chain and his master's furious commands to be quiet often drowned the rector's words.

The Captain had various eccentricities, especially where horses were concerned. He never sold one, being convinced that no one else would look after it properly. Those which were old, redundant, or had misbehaved in any way were out of luck. He personally shot them ('Can't trust those confounded vets – might miss …'), and caused elaborate tombstones to be erected over their graves. A hundred years hence, some wandering historian may wonder who Miss Crackenthorpe was, or Polly Hopkins, and why these unfortunate ladies were buried in a garden rather than a cemetery.

*

I'd hate to go back to when it took forty minutes to trot to Nenagh, but out riding, we didn't know how lucky we were as we trotted about the countryside with its clean air and almost deserted roads.

Hacking on the roads can be fairly hazardous now. No wonder that modern children sometimes look more as if they were going to play American football than go for a quiet ride along the road. Cars travel faster, tractors are much larger than they once were and plastic is everywhere. Plastic bags are draped over every hedge after a spring gale, and every possible commodity is packaged in them. Lorries with huge flapping covers tear along country lanes, and rally drivers practise controlled skids on hairpin bends.

It occurs to me that each generation of horses is born with less fear than the one before. Just as our forbears would have had hysterics if they had found themselves in a modern jet plane, the horses of olden times almost fainted at the sight of a motor car. The car might be a little box-like thing, chugging along at fifteen miles an hour, but it could cause as much terror as a fire-breathing dragon.

Present-day horses are as blasé about traffic as present-day children are about air travel. The odd thing is that this should be the case even when the horse has been bred in some remote spot, seeing no traffic at all. Do they learn from their mothers that there is nothing to fear? I feel it may have something to do with the people who handle them. Expecting that a horse will shy is the surest way to make him do so.

I once took a horse for schooling, having been told nothing except that he was as green as a cabbage. I rode him for miles without mishap, wondering why he'd been sent to me. There wasn't much traffic, but what there was he ignored. Finally, I rode him right through the town. No problem.

Baffled, I asked his owner about him. She said he had shied her off more than once. A nervous rider, she used to dismount as soon as a car came in sight, and hold the horse's head until it had gone.

The next time I rode this horse, he was quite bad in traffic. He spooked and sidled and tried to turn round. I am sure this was because I now knew his history and was sending him messages of anxiety through the reins. This horse was sold soon after, and gave no trouble to his new owners, safe in their blissful ignorance.

*

In the hills near my home, the winding roads have for many years been popular with those who fancied their chances as rally drivers. One such was a young Englishman who, about fifty years back, decided to try out his new sports car on a mountain called Pallasmore. The car was a low-slung MG with a long bonnet with a strap round it. As the young man roared round a bend, he overtook an old man driving a binder; two horses on the pole, a third tied to the back. The effect of the MG's appearance was electric – the driver managed to pull it up, but the binder was away.

The three horses bolted almost a mile down a steep and winding hill. At the bottom was Carrickmadden Bridge, hardly wider than the binder and set at a slight angle. The old man, a fine horseman in his day, had been hanging on to the reins grimly, concentrating on steering his team. Never for a moment losing his head, he guided his horses safely across the bridge: the hard pull up the valley on the opposite side stopped them most effectively.

'I'm so terribly sorry,' said the young man.

What the old man said is not on record.

CHAPTER SIX

Unwillingly to School

The outbreak of the Second World War is constantly being recalled in books such as this by people who were children at the time. Many claim to have known at once that 'Nothing would ever be the same again' and to have been deeply worried about the outcome. I remember the radio announcement – at least, I think I do. The general feeling in our household was that Hitler was a Bad Man, therefore Germany couldn't possibly win. I doubt if this is how my parents really felt, but it was certainly comforting for me.

My father, like most of those who fought their way right through the 1914–1918 war, was reluctant to talk about it. I begged for gory stories in vain. He claimed that if a man stated that he had waded through blood, he generally turned out to have spent the war in Cornwall or Aberdeen.

In Ireland in 1939 we had plenty of meat and dairy produce, but oil, tea and other imported goods disappeared almost at once. There was of course a black market, but soon even this ran short of petrol coupons. As for clothing, I was a huge child and growing all the time. My mother made me a dress out of my bedroom curtains, while hand-me-downs were donated by friends and relations of various shapes and sizes, cut in the styles of a decade earlier.

There were few tractors in Ireland at that time, and our stately

Morris Oxford was one of the very few cars in this out-of-the-way area; even so, the absence of any kind of oil had a dramatic effect on everyday life.

We had plenty of horses, but our traps and harnesses were ancient and rotten. At first, there was a small ration of petrol; soon it stopped. During the 1940 invasion scare, all farmers were ordered to place obstacles in their larger fields to prevent planes from landing. What kind of obstacle wasn't specified. A neighbour, not wishing to impede his ploughing, erected a row of tall poles along the edge of a quarry. Our vehicles – a gig, a side-car and a brougham, looked old and neglected scattered about in our largest field. I doubt if they would have delayed an invasion for long. This was the brougham soon to be passed on to Captain Finch.

At that time, I was doing lessons at my own house with a girl of my age called Helen White. We were taught by Jenny O'Callaghan, a young woman who drove an Austin Seven. When the petrol went, so did she. I was almost ten at the time and it was the end of any regular education for me until the end of the war more than fours years later. My parents took it in turn to teach me for an hour or so at a time, and I was happy with the arrangement.

Most people prefer to teach subjects they are good at and my parents were no exception. They were both fond of poetry and well versed in literature, so I got double helpings of that subject. My mother taught me literature, French, botany, Scripture and geography: my father taught me literature, Latin, Euclid, astronomy and ancient history. Nobody taught me arithmetic, and history ended with the death of Queen Victoria. I learned geography from a book written before the First World War redefined boundaries and changed names, before Ireland was a free state. But it was my parents, not my later teachers, who taught me to appreciate the English language.

When I was fourteen and a half, my education had been gradually abandoned and I assumed I was now an adult. There had been a plan to send me to a boarding school in England – I used to have nightmares about it. Then, on VE-Day, in the middle of the school year, I was sent away to school in Dublin.

*

This is supposed to be a happy book, but it is also my own story. Adults who ought to know better have a nasty habit of saying, 'Your schooldays are the happiest of your life.' This may be true for some; not for me. I was intensely miserable for the two-and-a-half years that followed. Trained in the stiff-upper-lip school, I had learned never to complain. In fact, this was almost the end of me, as I failed to complain of a severe pain a couple of years later. A burst appendix was removed just in time.

It didn't occur to me to argue when the school brochure arrived, and I didn't even consider simply refusing to go. Now, I feel sure my parents would have removed me if they'd had any inkling of my misery, but they hadn't. I had received what seemed to me like a long prison sentence, undeserved and grossly unfair, but off I went without a word of protest.

The school, called Knockrabo, was then about six miles from Dublin. Now the area is built up. Possibly it was a good school. It was located in an enormous and viciously cold Palladian mansion of great historic interest. Our classrooms had Adam mantelpieces, floor-to-ceiling mirrors and double mahogany doors with cut-crystal handles. When I heard a few years ago that the house had been pulled down, I felt a pang of regret. When I was there, I would gladly have helped demolish it.

The school stood halfway up Mount Annville Road, almost country in those days, right opposite Mount Annville Convent. There was absolutely no fraternizing. Mount Annville was a traditional girls' school, and the girls went out in crocodile. Ours was a rough and ready establishment, with a remarkable amount of freedom for its day. We watched the crocodile scornfully from the branches of a giant cedar tree on the lawn.

Knockrabo was a PNEU school. I've forgotten the exact meaning of those initials, although I remember telling a new girl we were all illegitimate and the letters meant 'Parents never even understood'. 'I'm not illegitimate,' she wailed. 'You must be,' we said.

My problem was that I had been brought up in almost total

isolation from my own age group. I simply didn't know how teenage girls behaved or thought. In some ways, they seemed alarmingly mature and worldly wise (I was naïve to a degree), in other ways they were children. One of the reasons I was sent away was to detach me from my first boyfriend. I think if I'd boasted about this young man, I might have impressed the other girls, but I was mature enough not to. I was not mature enough to know when they were lying or how to ignore teasing.

As an only child, I'd missed out on the friendly ragging which helps to prepare one for life. I had one skin too few, took people too seriously and soon developed a major loss of self-esteem.

I did a test which showed me to have progressed as far as short division and was placed in Form IV B with ten-year-olds. I was also put in a dormitory with this age group. I suffered from a kind of mainly non-violent bullying, but my reading (*John Brown's Schooldays*, *Eric,* or *Little by Little*) had prepared me. YOU MUST NOT HIT SOMEONE YOUNGER THAN YOURSELF. YOU MUST NOT TELL. I didn't tell. In her wonderful novel *Cat's Eye*, Margaret Atwood describes the technique of my persecutors so exactly that I could hardly bear to read it, even now.

The school was tiny. In my first year there were fewer than twenty boarders, aged from six to seventeen. The six-year-old ran away, but only got as far as the bus stop. The teaching was good. With a teacher/pupil ratio of about four to one that could be expected. We took the Cambridge School Certificate and Irish was not taught. I got a good grounding in English history, but learned none of the history of my own country. The games mistress, Elinor Mathews, tried to interest us in Irish history, and was prepared to teach elementary Irish, but nobody learnt it. We might almost have been attending an English school. One of the reasons for this was that many of the boarders were from England or the north of Ireland, having been sent away for the duration of the war.

I passed my exams in due course, but my only scholastic record was an incredible 8 per cent in a maths exam. I don't think it was ever equalled. After that, piano practice was replaced by extra maths, but I never learned. This is odd, as I can do problems in my head. If you are going to buy a bunch of cattle and you know they weigh 325 kilos each and that a fair price would be £107.50 per hundred kilos, you have to be able to reckon quickly in the auction ring. To use a calculator brands you as a wimp or, worse, an agricultural adviser.

To say I was homesick at school is an understatement. I yearned for my home, family and animals. There were no home weekends or half-term holidays for me; petrol was still a problem and trains were slow and unpredictable. The other girls seemed to me – solitary and eccentric as I was – to be as alien as Martians. Naturally they disliked me. I made only one real friend, and she left to complete her education in England.

Some of the girls went for weekly riding lessons with the late Colonel Joe Hume Dudgeon, an international horseman of great repute. I didn't go because my father taught me at home. He was an excellent horseman and a high-handicap polo-player in his day. Unlike many army men of his generation, he was practical rather than hidebound. For example, he didn't teach me to mount facing the horse's tail. He held that, with a green horse, and all of mine were green, you should keep your eye on the front end and to hell with the book. I appreciated my father's teaching, but it didn't stop me from being green with envy as I watched the others going off for their riding lessons.

The Dudgeon horses were far removed from riding-school hacks, except for the wooden-quiet ponies provided for beginners. One of the horses was a winner of the Irish St Leger called Ochiltree. At that time a racehorse, if a gelding, had little value once he stopped winning. We used to see Reynoldstown, a dual winner of the Grand National, pulling a dog-cart in Dundrum.

The winter of 1948 was the worst since records began. In Ireland, we weren't used to hard weather or prepared for heavy snow, so there was total chaos in the cities, and country places were cut off without supplies. Most of the pupils were sent home, but I was one of half a dozen with measles. We, and a skeleton staff, stayed on.

As we recovered and could have gone home, the blizzards returned and we were cut off from supplies of milk, coal and bread. The only plentiful food was cornflakes, flour and dried apricots. The power lines collapsed and left us in the dark. We had to stay in bed in order to keep warm. It was a week before the avenue was cleared.

*

The high spot of the summer for me occurred when another girl and I were allowed into Dublin for the day with the housekeeper. This housekeeper was an attractive girl, only a few years older than we were, and equally impatient of authority. Instead of shopping – difficult on 10 shillings a term – we went to Phoenix Park races.

I was ferociously bitten by a flea on the bus, and it seemed as good a reason as any to put two weeks' pocket money on a two year old, hideously named 'The Bug'. The horse duly obliged at 7/1 and I spent the rest of the day losing my winnings piecemeal and scratching.

Back at school, we used to bet on the Grand National, giving our pennies and sixpences to Cooney, the odd-job man who laid our bets for us. The first post-war race was won by Lovely Cottage, and a girl who lived in one backed him. Most of us went for the great Prince Regent who, having been in training when the race was in abeyance, must have been one of the best horses not to win a National. Prince Regent was clobbered with weight that year and the next, still being placed both times. The second time we had learned caution and hedged our bets.

One girl gave Cooney a shilling to put on Caughoo, because she had a cold and the name sounded like a sneeze. Cooney backed a better-fancied horse for her, because Caughoo was at 100/1 and he didn't want to throw away a schoolgirl's pocket money. But Caughoo won.

*

The PNEU system does not encourage the competitive spirit. I never quite understood the principle of this, but I think it is akin to being virtuous for virtue's sake, rather than because of a fear of hell fire. One was expected to do one's best without being given marks, good or bad. 'Remarks', which were used instead, ran in descending order from excellent to unsatisfactory. Games, however, couldn't be org-

[40]

anized along these lines, and we were terrors on the hockey field and the netball pitch. After matches with other schools, we would travel back on the bus, proudly displaying our wounds. Black eyes and hacked shins were all in a day's work. We were considered very tough for Protestants. Hockey is a rough game, and roughest when played by convent girls, whose games mistresses were nuns. I particularly remember the fighting tactics of the girls of St Mary's, Haddington Road.

I think the competitive spirit is built-in rather than acquired. Something primitive to do with survival, I daresay. I know that it is addictive. A love of racing is part of this fondness for competition and it too is addictive. And I'm not talking about compulsive gambling. From childhood games like tag and hide-and-seek, the racing addict proceeds by way of bicycles to greyhounds, fast cars or horses. I, along with some of my companions at school, became addicted to snail-racing.

The craze started when we all backed Prince Regent to win at Leopardstown. We hadn't much knowledge of betting, except that if the horse won, so would we. The Prince won at long odds on and our sixpences were turned into sevenpences. Disillusioned, we decided on a new sport, betting to be limited to a sweepstake and to be organized by ourselves.

We collected our snails at the bottom of the garden, and transferred them to their training quarters in the Domestic Science kitchen. There, we raced them along teatrays towards a dish of lettuce. As they tended to stop and fight – or fraternize, it was hard to tell which – we erected rulers and raced them along tracks.

We painted their shells in our racing colours. Mine wore light blue and claret hoops on his (or possibly her) shell. The fastest snail, a very large specimen called Semolina, was owned and trained by a girl called Maeve Dring. She – Semolina, that is – was bright blue with black spots, and her track record was twenty-four inches in twelve minutes, or two inches a minute.

After a while, the headmistress discovered what we were up to in the Domestic Science kitchen. Was she relieved? No. The snails were banished and we were told off for cruelty to animals. In vain we pleaded that the snails loved racing and that the training was all done by kindness. We were ordered to release them in the wild or, more precisely, at the bottom of the tennis court.

Now comes the part you won't believe, but it's true. About a fortnight later, at prayers, one of us was pounding out a hymn on the grand piano and the rest of us were singing. Suddenly I noticed a large, bright blue snail with black spots clinging to the leg of the piano. Semolina had come home.

A day or two later, I found my own snail climbing up the wall of the house towards the same window that Semolina must have used. By degrees, five out of the stable of eleven came home. They had travelled, hedge and dyke so to speak, all of 150 yards.

Those of us who are afflicted by the racing bug will match anything that has legs or wheels or, in extreme cases, creatures that have neither.

*

At home in the holidays, I went to the street fairs in Nenagh and watched my father buying and selling cattle. He encouraged me to help and taught me a great deal about judging and dealing. I can't imagine where he got his own judgment, having come to farming at more than fifty years old, but he made few mistakes. In the Easter holidays, when I was sixteen, he was sick in bed and sent me to the fair on my bicycle with an ashplant and two blank cheques, to buy twenty bullocks.

I cycled into the town, where every street was packed with buyers, sellers and cattle. I was terrified. The cattle, twenty shorthorn bullocks, cost £18 each, and I spent so much time sorting and choosing them that I feel I might still recognize one of them today. When I got home, I got £2 commission. In the autumn I was given the job of selling the same cattle, which did well and earned me another £2. Going back to school was worse than before.

Towards the end of my time at school, I had to make up my mind whether I wanted to go to university and try for a degree in modern languages, or to go home and be a working farmer. I hadn't any choice really, as my father was unwell and would have sold the family place if he'd had nobody to succeed him there. Already I was buying and selling cattle for him in my school holidays. I went home.

CHAPTER SEVEN

Beginner's Luck

I was just seventeen when I left school, and I found life down on the farm pretty boring. I'd imagined I'd have some say in the running of the place, but my father's health had suddenly improved (he lived another ten years), so I was still no more than cheap labour. I thought of ways to save time and work, but they found no favour. My work was mostly with the livestock, partly because I liked animals better than machinery, partly because I could run. My God, how I ran. It was some time before it occurred to me, as I sprinted after some wayward heifers, that I wasn't even the under cow-girl or assistant carter. I was the dog.

There was a short interlude when having won a place in art college, I took it up for one term. The place was for Dublin, but my mother had been brought up in Surrey and thought it would be nice for me to stay with one of my aunts. The Dublin College of Art had a reciprocal agreement with Guilford Art School, so that was where I was sent. Rationing was at its worst and I felt bad about eating the food, and conscious of my healthy weight. Two-thirds of the students were adult men, demobbed from the forces. I was in the same year as Elizabeth Frink, and we both idled and drew horses on any piece of blank paper we could find. I didn't learn much and what I did learn wasn't art. Then my father had a relapse and home I went again. I wasn't at all nervous of buying and selling stock after my earlier experiences, but again I expected to be given more say in the running of the farm, which was losing money fast. In wartime you could hardly help making some profit; now Irish wheat and beef no longer fetched premium prices. Paddy, Edmund and John (nicknamed Rowdy) were loyal, genuine and determined that nothing should change. Their wages were low but had to be found somehow; they had spent all their working lives at Crannagh and would stay until they retired. I wondered how the hell we would make ends meet.

I longed to buy and sell horses, perhaps on commission as I had no money of my own, but, naturally enough, nobody felt like trusting me to buy one for them. I had my own horse, Matilda, but she was mine only on condition that she was available if needed for work on the farm. Still I was certain that I could make enough money out of horses to prop up the farm, pay the wages and give me a living too, if only I could lay my hands on some capital.

I didn't want to go back to art college but the life of a farm labourer wasn't alluring. Cattle were bought only twice a year. I stayed at home and broke in carthorses for peanuts.

Then my uncle died. I'd been very fond of Uncle Algy, but was surprised to hear that he'd left me 'one hundred pounds in cash, to spend as she thinks fit'. Mind you, I don't suppose he thought I'd get my legacy as soon as I left school; he died comparatively young. My relations thought it wildly imprudent to allow me the use of all that money. I sometimes wondered exactly what they expected me to do with it.

Among the pinnacles in my life was the day when my father gave me the money in crisp new tenners. He thought the idea was very sensible and didn't even suggest the Post Office or the 3 per cent War Loan.

I bought two bullocks for £25 each and a horse for £50. I collected a £2 luckpenny on the horse, which I spent on a bridle for her. From that day on I was self-supporting.

*

Talk about beginner's luck! I bought the bullocks first and they doubled their money. I bought three with what they made. Meanwhile I had turned my attention to buying a horse. About five miles away there was a hill farm owned by a man called John O'Sullivan, locally known as 'The Millionaire'. He showed no outward sign of wealth, but I had often noticed his horses when I was out hunting. They were two exceptional grey Irish draught mares, either of which would carry off prizes at Millstreet today. They were a mother and daughter team, and it was a pleasure to see them working together. Both were breeding regularly to the thoroughbred sire Turbulent, who stood down in County Clare. The younger mare produced a noted heavy-weight showhunter by him; the younger, Arizona, was dam of a three- year-old filly which I determined to buy.

I set off straight away, riding my bike and carrying a rope. Even then I wasn't quite green enough to let The Millionaire see the rope; I hid it under a gorse bush near his gate. I think he asked me £75. I know I bid him £40. Judging by later dealings, that £40 would have bought her. I parted with £50, got my luckpenny and went back to collect the rope.

I should have called this book, like Jack Yeats's, *The Charmed Life*. Why didn't that horse knock me off my bike as I freewheeled down the steep hill while she cantered beside me? She was quite unbroken. I'd been training stiff-legged carthorses and when I think of the stupid things I did around that time, I shiver. But nothing happened. I thought the filly deserved a fine name, so I called her after the nearest village, Ballycarrido. After a while it seemed like a less good idea and while I had her she was called Sally.

I set to work to improvise breaking tackle out of rotting trap harness and pieces of rope. Sally broke them with scornful ease. I dispensed with tackle and used a blinker bridle and plough lines instead. Broken and hunted, she grew into a nice big mare and had a wonderful temperament.

When I felt the time was ripe to sell Sally, I advertised her in *The Irish Field*. I had one reply, a letter which appeared to be signed Olive Plunkett. I replied, 'Dear Miss Plunkett ...' I don't know why I opted for Miss rather than Mrs. This person's next letter was signed, 'Yours sincerely, Miss Plunkett.' This seemed unusual but not extra-ordinary. More letters passed. Miss Plunkett came to see Sally. I opened the door to a tall grey-haired man of seventy-odd.

'I'm Miss Plunkett,' he said.

In my defence, I should point out that I was a shy, awkward teenager. 'I was expecting a hatchet-faced elderly woman,' I blurted out.

'So was I,' said 'Miss' Plunkett. It was a good ice-breaker. I hadn't seen the 'r' on the end of Oliver.

I got £125 for Sally and bought a Connemara pony, another horse, a set of breaking tackle, an extra bullock and a gramophone. There wasn't anything over for records.

Sally was a great success with 'Miss' Plunkett, who was a retired colonial judge. He hunted her and she later won prizes in Dublin as a brood mare.

*

Sally's successor, Marigold, was totally different. A showy, bright chestnut, she was, like Sally, unbroken and, like her, about 16.1 hands. There the resemblance ended. Mind you, I'd been warned. I'd been told more than once that I couldn't expect to have any luck with a horse bought from a rate collector.

Marigold, who cost £55, was a little back at the knees, otherwise she was hard to fault – on confirmation. Breaking her in was some-thing else. I had cause to be glad I'd learned to fall on my feet. By degrees, I learned the signs of approaching trouble. When Marigold's ears were pricked, one of them bent forward at a sharper angle than the other. When she was contemplating mischief, this ear tipped still farther forward. I have never seen another horse with ears like this, and I advise nervous types to avoid them.

Marigold's dam was by a classically bred country sire called Prophet's Thumb. He carried the 'Prophet's thumb-mark,' a deep dent in the muscle of the neck. Mahomet, we are told, marked his favourite stallion by pressing his thumb against its neck. The thumb left a mark which has been handed down to direct descendants of the stallion. Commoner in Arabians than in thoroughbreds, it is said to be a lucky mark. Marigold carried the mark, and even those who thought she couldn't survive having belonged to a rate collector felt that the thumb-mark might avert bad luck.

I was learning patience and even a little caution. I took my time with Marigold and, after a few weeks, was able to ride her on the road without trouble. In the stable, she had a habit of whipping round, showing the white at the tops of her eyes – a sign of fear rather than temper. To prove the point, I could hear her heart thudding.

One day, Marigold was drinking at the trough outside the back door, while I held the rope, daydreaming as usual. I think she must have been stung by a bee. If she had been attacked by a tiger, she couldn't have reacted any more violently. I found myself in the water trough, without any clear idea of how I'd got there. I could hear Marigold galloping hard in the distance. I picked myself out of the water and followed.

Marigold had done a complete circuit of the farm, jumping one gate and smashing three. She finished by galloping headlong into a thick hedge, and how she didn't blind herself or break her neck I can't think. She was limping (so was I), bleeding from half a dozen cuts, had pulled off two of her shoes and acquired a big knee which never quite returned to normal. I picked up her saddle, its girths broken, on the avenue.

Marigold wasn't rideable for a month, so I put her back in long reins and drove her about, which did her all the good in the world.

Years afterwards, I noticed that all the quiet horses I bought had hard mouths, while the awkward customers had mouths like silk. The reason of course is that nobody is in a hurry to start riding a nervy animal with a cold back, while the quiet ones are often ridden before their mouths are half made. Anyway, Marigold responded to her second breaking and I rode and even hunted her without any more bother. I advertised her ('suit competent rider'), and didn't get any replies at all.

*

While I was having problems with Marigold, I'd sold the pony and bullocks for profit and bought four bullocks and a cob. I also rented a field to put them in, and even bought some gramophone records. But I had £55 tied up in Marigold and no customers. I took her to Limerick fair.

This was my first fair and I enquired when it would be. 'The Tuesday before the last Friday,' I was told. This curious timing had a reason. A quarterly cattle fair was held the last Friday of January, April, July and October. The horse fair took place the previous Tuesday.

The early train to Limerick had a number of horse-boxes and cattle-wagons attached. Marigold was to travel in a railway horse-box. The horses were supposed to be tied up, three abreast, to iron mangers. Vast oily black headcollars were provided, each with three mighty chains, every one capable of anchoring an elephant. I preferred to travel in the groom's compartment, holding the reins through the hatch.

At Limerick, we unloaded the horses among the passengers and I joined twenty or thirty others in a ride through the city to the fair green, where we were swallowed up by the crowd. The green, now built over, provided plenty of space for galloping. My first impression was of horses galloping in every direction. A coped wall divided the green from the cemetery, and was occasionally used as a jump, although its height deterred all but the bravest. Farther down, near the main gates, men and horses were packed like sardines. There was a charge of half a crown to go in. If they were all paid for, which I doubt, the fair must have been a money-spinner.

Marigold was not a money-spinner. She made more than she cost, a different thing from making profit. At least expenses were low. Her train fare in today's money was 75p.

To a newcomer, the whole thing was a wild, orderless jumble. I was at an advantage, compared with other beginners, because I was used to buying and selling cattle in the street fairs. I wasn't intimidated by the shouting, jostling throng. In fact, it had much in common with a cattle fair as some of the young horses were driven there in droves of up to twenty. The youngsters were called 'long-tails'. Often the end of the tail was tied in a knot.

Having sold Marigold, I was free to look around for a replacement. I soon discovered that it was a buyer's market and I made up my mind that in future I'd buy in the fairs and sell at home. When horses were plentiful and cheap, it wasn't so much getting a good price as 'getting rid', and buying something even cheaper. Those who dealt in numbers employed 'blockers' to cut out suitable animals, engage their owners in conversation and, if possible, to lure them away to some lane or yard until the dealer had time to come and inspect them.

I evaded the blockers instinctively, and sold Marigold to a Yorkshire dealer. She went to the Bramham Moor Hunt and led a reformed life thereafter.

*

While I have never made much money from buying horses off the land and selling them in fairs (who has?), it was selling in fairs that got me valuable contacts which enabled me to buy for the Swiss Cavalry and various British police forces. After I'd sold a few horses to dealers in the fairs, I was able to persuade them to buy from me at home. This was better for me and better for them too. They were able to take their time in making a choice and to try the horses out.

At that first Limerick fair, I saw a group of men gazing up the road with the utmost intensity. 'What are you doing?' I asked.

'Waiting for Grantham,' they said. I was no wiser. I didn't know that Tommy Grantham from Sussex was the best buyer of ridden horses travelling to the fairs. His presence or absence had a considerable effect on the trade. Sellers prayed that he'd come; buyers hoped he'd be taken ill or miss the boat. On this occasion, the group waited in vain.

At the railway station, wagons waited which had been booked by dealers, each with the dealer's name chalked on the side. There were quite a number at Limerick, but when I went to Cahirmee for the first time, it was an eye-opener for me – wagons stretched as far as the eye could see. No fewer than twelve had GRANTHAM chalked on the side. There and then I resolved that some day it would be worth my while to book a wagon for myself, with my name, SMITHWICK, chalked on the side. The opportunity came within two years and I went down to the station on some trumped-up excuse, but really to gloat over my wagon.

The porter, though, had forgotten my name. There it stood with TIPPERARY WOMAN chalked on its side. Oh well.

*

When I started horse-dealing, I began to think about luck in what I suppose you might call a constructive way. It was always being mentioned: 'the luck of the Irish', 'the Devil's own luck' ... I encountered all sorts of superstitions, which I brushed aside; later I began to have reservations.

Most Irish people believe firmly in luck. Country people still say 'Good luck', rather than 'Goodbye'. There is such a thing, but it's too often confused with ability. There are few things more irritating than to be congratulated on your good fortune just when you are thinking how clever you've been. On the other hand, it's comforting when your laziness or stupidity are attributed to bad luck. Most infuriating is the well-wisher who is always at hand when you wake up in hospital to tell you how lucky you are to be alive. If you'd been lucky you wouldn't be there.

In horse-dealing circles, belief in luck is particularly strong. 'Cutting one's lucky' is old fairground cant for going away. And we all know about luckpennies and the regrettable habit of spitting on them.

The original luckpenny was a copper coin with a hole in it. Then the term began to stand for a few pence or some loose change, given by the seller 'to make the horse lucky'. Now it's a mere bargaining handle. You hear of deals for sums like £2000 and £500 for luck – 25 per cent of the price. This may be so that a cheque for the supposed full amount can be shown to the sceptical.

In one instance, the luckpenny was the opposite. A dodgy dealer paid for a horse with a large cheque and collected £50 luck in cash. The cheque bounced ...

I sometimes saw a character who had a double-headed penny. He worked with a stooge who could be relied on to call 'heads'. The two would decide on a hefty amount for luck, then toss double or nothing. One day, they tried this trick with a man who was certain that an English penny couldn't possibly bring anyone luck. 'I want none of your heads and tails,' he roared, 'I call hens or harps.' This was pre-decimal, and he produced an old Irish penny with the hen and chickens on one side and the harp on the other. I'd like to be able to record that he won the toss, but he didn't.

Good-luck charms are getting uncommon, and so is the carrying out of lucky practices. One of these is always to dress your left leg first. If you neglect this simple precaution, or forget it, don't think you can avert your ill fortune by undressing and starting again. Your luck is out for the day and you would be wise to stay at home.

CHAPTER EIGHT

Going to the Dogs

I may have given the impression that, from the time I bought Sally, my life was given over to horse-dealing. It wasn't; it took years to build up a business and I'd no money for anything else. The years between the legacy and my father's death were spent working on the farm, training horses and trying to improve the family fortunes. My only relaxation was foxhunting.

Foxhunting, did I say? It used to be more of a joke than a sport when I started to take part, having acquired Pippin. I was about ten, the war was on, there was no petrol, so no trailers, and cars were confined to priests, doctors and a few favoured mortals thought to be indispensable. It was nothing to hack twelve miles to a meet, and Pippin was never shod in all the years I owned her. Her hooves were so hard that, when we did try to shoe her, they turned the nails like drawing-pins.

Our hounds were transported to the more distant meets in a 'dray car and truck', a high-sided farm cart, which held four couple of hounds. The whipper-in drove one of the hunt horses between the shafts, the huntsman rode the other.

My earliest hunting memories are of gallops from pub to pub rather than across country. My job was to wait outside, holding the drinkers' horses, and very boring it was. I was rewarded with boiled sweets or, my favourites, those square, shiny affairs called satin cushions.

The hunting could hardly have been classed as a blood sport, even by the most tender-hearted. Foxes were scarce and we seldom found, let alone killed one. The hunt had neither a master nor any money. Sometimes we didn't even have a huntsman. When this happened, eager volunteers would bring the pack to the meet, and it would be 'hunted' by anyone who felt like having a go. No wonder they didn't perform very well. I remember a group of us passing a horn from hand to hand, each trying in turn and in vain to extract the right sort of noise from it. Our inefficiency can be judged from the remark of a would-be huntsman in cover, 'Jesus, lads, we're ruined now, they've found a fox.'

After a few seasons, the hunt's finances improved and we acquired a master, some new hounds and the status of foxhounds. Previously, we'd been classed as harriers, although we didn't hunt hares except occasionally by mistake. I was proud of my harrier coat, given me by our former huntsman. It was a mouldy blackish green with silver buttons, and skirts which almost reached my ankles.

There is an idea that fifty-odd years ago Irish farmers were too poor to hunt. In fact, there was a far higher ratio of hunting farmers than there is now. Because so many hunted, it was rarely that we were met with oaths and pitchforks – anyway we knew where this might happen and didn't go looking for trouble. It was only when incomes began to increase and with them the snobbery of the haves and have-nots, that people in my area began to go hunting because it was 'the thing to do'. And that attitude is guaranteed to kill any sport stone dead.

*

Hunting from pub to pub took on a new dimension on public holidays, especially St Stephen's Day – or Boxing Day, according to the country of your birth.

It is a great day for having a good time, a good way of propelling the children out of doors with the assurance that they will enjoy the fresh air; an opportunity to make do with turkey sandwiches instead of preparing yet another dinner. It is the only occasion I can think of when respectable elderly men and women run across other people's fields, yelling their heads off, without the risk of being certified insane.

My father, a moderate man, welcomed the hunt except on St Stephen's Day – or Stephenses Day as it is called hereabouts. 'You can come hunting as often as you like,' he told the master of the time, 'but if you want to play Cowboys and Indians, you can do it somewhere else.'

If our normal sport featured gallops from pub to pub, Stephenses Day was for many the pub without the gallop. For some, it still is. On one such day, two worthy members challenged one another to a race. This ended with a horrifying collision at top speed. Back to the pub. Outside that same pub, a gentleman who normally knew better was seen to mount his horse facing the tail. 'Something wrong,' he muttered. 'No ears.'

Long ago, the local paper boasted a sporting correspondent who wrote a column about our goings-on every week. When describing the St Stephen's Day meet, he really spread himself. 'Nature,' he said, 'was clad in her gayest festoonery.' Sometimes he broke into verse, and I remember the lines,

> There is an empty saddle on yon hillside
> Another seeks its rider in the vale.

Empty saddles were certainly a feature of the day, although they usually behaved in a more conventional way, with their riders seeking them. Catching horses was often my task. Children out hunting were considered a nuisance to be endured unless they made themselves useful, so very few children went out. Sometimes there were no children about, like the time when the master's horse shot him off into a ditch full of water with a last-second refusal. 'Catch that bloody horse!' screamed the master at a harmless-looking foot-follower, as he hauled himself out of the water. The foot-follower ran off as fast as he could, caught the horse, mounted it, set it at the stream, jumped across and followed the receding pack out of sight.

Some hours later, he handed it over to somebody else and prudently went home.

'Foxes have died in countless braces, but the hunt goes on,' stated *The Nenagh Guardian*. They may have done, but I doubt if the hounds had much to do with it. I think most foxes died of natural causes such as old age. Certainly on St Stephen's Day they were safe. The din made by the approaching sportsmen warned all foxes of normal intelligence to get underground and stay there.

Another feature of holiday meets was the extraordinary variety of dress worn by the followers. Convention was thrown to the winds at Christmas. Yellow oilskin macs with pull-ups, woolly hats, galoshes with spurs (yes, really), anything went.

> The fox, as we know, is devoted to sport.
> He likes being hunted and loves being caught
> And eaten, but pity his bitter distress
> When those who pursue him don't know how to dress.

For years, hard hats were the exception, most men hunting bareheaded. In a snapshot dated 1951, more than half are hatless. I once lent a green three-year-old to a young man, and begged him to wear a hard hat, but he waved it away. Later I found him sitting in the middle of the road, gingerly fingering an egg-sized lump on his head. I sympathized, but said he must wear the hat if he rode my horse again. 'What kind of a sissy do you take me for?' he demanded angrily.

*

My fondness for hunting didn't really extend to foxhounds, which I always felt were pretty stupid once separated from their companions. Now that I have been breeding, working and often writing about Border Collies for thirty-five years, I'm often assured that I must be 'a great dog-lover'. What, I wonder, is a dog-lover? It must be impossible to love the whole canine race, Chihuahua and bull mastiff alike. I like dogs – deserving dogs, that is – and a few have meant more to me than most humans, but I don't care to be labelled 'dog-lover' or to be labelled at all for that matter.

That said, I must admit that even the most cynical can be won over by a litter of cuddly puppies. Strong men drool and go '... a-a-aaah ...'. I have learned to be more impressed by a responsible attitude towards adult dogs, having seen too many spoilt puppies grow into spoilt dogs.

Nothing could be more spoilable than a six-week-old foxhound puppy, all silky skin, floppy ears, appealing expression. I have reared dozens, but the two that stick in my mind were called Tearful and Terrible.

Young foxhounds, like young guide dogs, are 'put out to walk' for most of their first year. They go to farm homes where they get good food, individual attention and, with luck, some basic obedience training. At the time when I was training Sally, Tearful and Terrible were about six months old. (These are not usual names, by the way. All the litter had to have names starting with T-E. My friend got Teaspoon and Temper.)

To anyone used to collies, foxhounds seem totally brainless. They aren't, but their limited intelligence is designed for working within a pack. A single hound sticks close to his master's heels because he fears being left alone, or having to make a decision for himself.

Tearful and Terrible followed me about like a couple of substantial and hungry shadows. Forgetting that the huntsman might not thank me, I taught Terrible to retrieve, and both of them to fetch the cows. I had been the dog for too long. They were slow learners, but re-membered what they'd been taught. They never learned to nip the cows' heels, but what they lacked in force, they made up for with noise. Their yowling sent the cows running for their lives and the milk yield plummeted.

When the puppies had been returned to the kennels, they won a prize for best couple at the puppy show. I received a gilt powder compact, engraved TEARFUL *** TERRIBLE 1948. I still have it, and wonder what a stranger would make of the inscription. I was again dogless and running after the cattle myself.

I tried to train various mongrel terriers to work, with no success. Nowadays, as a breeder of pedigree dogs, I find myself adopting a lofty attitude towards mongrels. Indeed, some of them are ugly, stupid and ill-behaved, but then, so are some of their blue-blooded owners. Many people who've owned a clever mongrel say, 'All mongrels are clever.' This is like marrying a sincere man and saying, 'All men are sincere.' Personal experience isn't always a reliable guide.

I've owned mongrels which were clever and mongrels which were thick. Two were among the brightest dogs I've known, but their minds didn't work like a collie's. Working dogs are bred to obedience and only anticipate an order in a crisis. A working dog which thinks it knows better than its handler is too clever by half. Better than being stupid, though.

*

I've received some original luckpennies, including a sack of potatoes and two tickets for a dance in Skibbereen. Another was a puppy. I was buying Connemaras to go to England, and one of them was rather expensive, so I asked for an extra luckpenny. The owner of the pony said, 'I'll give you a luckpenny you'll never forget.' With that, he moved some rocks which were blocking the door of a shed, shot back two heavy bolts, inched the door open and called, 'Here, Tiger!'

I waited nervously for a Doberman or Rottweiler to rush out. A tiny straw-coloured puppy emerged unsteadily and stood blinking in the light. His coat felt like poor-quality Draylon and he sat on the palm of my hand and growled at me. I laughed and put him in the pocket of my mackintosh. Then I mounted the pony and rode home.

In addition to the raincoat, I was wearing heavy cords and the type of underwear charitably called 'sensible'. Tiger gnawed his way through the lot and, when he reached my leg, he kept right on gnawing. In the other pocket, I had a note the farmer had given me with TIGER written on it – as if I could forget. It was torn off a letter and on the back was printed, Gabriel Aloysius Brook. I have no idea who this fine-sounding person is, or was, and we used to joke about it, saying it was Tiger's show-ring name.

Tiger grew into a smart little dog, rather like a Finnish Spitz but much smaller. In addition to being a discriminating watchdog, he fetched the cows, retrieved small game and could run down and catch a rabbit in the open. In fact, he combined the best of half-a-dozen breeds and was a gentle, intelligent companion. Out walking, he noticed that I picked up sweetpapers and cigarette packets dropped in the fields and put them in the dustbin. When I was driving the tractor, Tiger spent hours collecting litter and stacking it neatly by the bin. When I picked mushrooms, he ran ahead and barked if he found one. When I was ill, he fetched boots and hats to encourage me to go out. Ordered to desist, he levered a book out of the shelf and brought me that instead.

He was a one-woman dog – I thought. When Tiger was old and going blind, I got engaged. He refused to be won over by my fiancé, never growling at him, but turning his back and walking away with some dignity. He then transferred his affection from me to my mother, who was delighted. Before, he had accepted her only as a substitute when I was away. I think he was not so much jealous as bitterly offended. Evidently, he thought I was repaying thirteen years of selfless devotion with a shabby trick.

Tiger never relented. For the last two years of his life, he treated my husband and myself alike with polite indifference. I pretended I didn't mind, but I did.

CHAPTER NINE

The Life of Riley

After the war, the leap into the past was reversed, petrol and oil seemed to return in a flash, along with tea, oranges, coffee and other sorely missed commodities.

Horses disappeared as quickly from the farms as from the roads, and the countryside appeared to sprout little grey Ferguson tractors like mushrooms. By the standards of those days they were fine and I learned to drive a tractor on one of them, lent by a kind neighbour. Another proud owner of a 'Grey Fergie' went so far as to send his pony to the factory and personally chop up his trap for firewood the very day the first post-war petrol tanker came to town.

His action turned out to have been premature. Like thousands of others, his car had been up on blocks in the garage for five years. It refused to start and, when it did, the tyres burst one after another. New tyres had not yet reappeared. We smiled to ourselves as we watched him crossly cycling into town.

Our old Morris had survived better, but some mice had eaten the insulation off the wires under the bonnet. My father, always resourceful, separated the bare bits carefully, keeping them apart with non-conducting material – sods of turf. Then he drove the car to the garage for servicing.

One of the mechanics 'borrowed' the car to go out that night. It stopped and he looked under the bonnet where he was surprised to find a number of sods of turf. He removed these and drove on. Later, he switched on the lights. The explosion that followed sent him careering into a deep ditch. As they say, you can't beat the old horse.

Horses whose owners liked a drink or two regularly found their way home without much help from their drivers. Many of those horses knew which pub to stop at. A farmer from this parish used to spend a considerable amount of time and money at Nolan's Bar. He drove there in a trap drawn by a grey mare. His wife stayed at home. When this farmer got the 'flu, his wife harnessed the grey mare and drove to town to fetch the doctor. The mare trotted slowly but with determination up to the door of Nolan's Bar, where she stopped. Nothing would induce her to go any farther, and the lady had to leave her there and seek the doctor on foot. Later, after a suitable interval, the mare consented to turn and trot gently home.

I acquired a little car after I had been horse-dealing long enough to pay for it, but a tractor was still vetoed. Neither of the two workmen drove one and neither was young, said my father. True, my horses were paying better than the farm, so my time was better spent at the fairs, but I seldom wasted that time arguing with my father.

I borrowed my neighbour's little grey Fergie again and tried to teach Paddy to drive it. He sat on it while I got it started, showed him the controls and got him to press the clutch pedal as I put it in low bottom gear. This would produce a speed of about two miles an hour. I instructed Paddy to raise his foot gently and stood back.

With a slight – a very slight – jerk, the tractor moved forward and set off at a crawl. Exclaiming, 'Jesus, Mary and Joseph!' Paddy jumped down and could neither be threatened nor coaxed into getting back in the seat. Eventually, Edmund learned how to drive and he – I can't imagine how – taught Paddy, who became a reasonably good driver. He sometimes shouted at the tractor at first, but he never did anything stupid with it, unlike myself.

*

I couldn't go on borrowing from my neighbours, and my horse-dealing left less and less time for following farm horses. I decided to hire from the garage. I was the only person insured to drive those tractors and there were many occasions when the insurance companies narrowly escaped large claims. Some had no brakes, others had strange steering, the drive shafts were never protected and one of them went on fire twice. (These were minor fires, quenched with a wet sack.)

I remember a huge orange Ford van which had to be primed with petrol, poured in out of a jug, and which had only two usable forward gears – bottom and top. As it had no governor, it was possible to drive it at thirty miles an hour along the road. Just a little better was an old, battered David Brown, another big machine. This was the last I hired before buying one of my own. It was a late harvest, before the general use of combines in this area, and we were drawing in the last of the wheat when Ballinasloe fair came round, on the first Sunday in October.

I had been working hard, stooking then pitching corn and, between times, buying and selling horses. I still had some standing wheat and decided to get it combined. Combines were rare, but there was one, which arrived on Sunday, the fair day. It was hard in those days to get people to work on a Sunday and I had orders for two horses. That day we worked until midnight, and the next I took three loads of corn to town on a borrowed trailer attached to the brakeless David Brown. On both days I took time off for a frantic dash to Ballinasloe – forty miles – and was luckily able to find suitable horses.

I set off with the last load of corn in a great hurry on Monday evening, because the grain-merchants' store would soon be closing. The corn was all in bags, and the trailer a flat one whose drawbar was a length of railway line, rightly discarded. The tractor roared along at a great rate, but steering it was something else. The method was to spin the wheel and wait. Eventually, the cogs would engage with an agonizing jolt. After a day of this, one of my wrists swelled so much that I had to cut my shirtsleeve open.

I backed my load into the bay a few minutes before closing time, with apologies. 'Don't hang about, get on with it,' I was told.

At that moment, the dodgy railway line snapped and down came the trailer, yards from the intake point and blocking the long alley which was the only way in – or out. I doubt if I have ever been less popular, and it was night again before everything was sorted out. I got a breakdown gang to shift the trailer, drove home in the dark (I need hardly say the tractor had no lights) and went to bed.

Early next morning I returned from the garage with another borrowed trailer, smaller but sounder, and found a customer for one of my Ballinasloe horses having breakfast with my mother while he waited for me. I gave him some sort of show with the horse over a few jumps and he bought it. 'You must have the life of Riley,' he said. 'Nothing to do only canter around on a horse all day.'

I agreed that I had.

*

Life wasn't all buying and selling horses and cattle in my early farming days. I of course had to grow crops. The war years had seen a boom when you could throw any kind of wheat into a bag and it would end up as flour – optimistically called white.

A friend of my mother's was the only person who still had white soda-bread on her table and she explained that her cook sieved the flour. Sieving it at our house only resulted in beige flour instead of brown. My mother asked the cook in question what she sieved it through. 'One of my stockings,' she said.

We had ploughed out a lot of extra land, bought extra horses and paid extra labour in order to produce more wheat. Modern strains of wheat ripen early – haytime and harvest overlap. When I was growing wheat, it ripened in mid-September, or, if the weather was unkind, even later. Stooks could be seen sprouting green ears of corn in the fields in November at times. Times got very hard in the early fifties, when I was trying, in order to please my father, to indicate to Paddy, Edmund and John what I wanted without giving any orders, and making a living.

In April 1958 my father died, after a desperate illness lasting about three months. My mother was by then a bad asthmatic and I had to try my hand at nursing. My father wouldn't hear of a hospital although he grumbled about my methods. 'You're not dosing a bullock,' he would say. Neither would he allow anyone else to look after him. My mother couldn't possibly heave a big, heavy man about. I could and did. For the last fortnight I don't think I left the house once.

The summer which followed was one of the worst on record. The farm was understocked, overstaffed and had long since ceased to be a paying enterprise. I had hastily ploughed out an extra ten acres and sown it with wheat in order to meet my commitments. It was ready in mid-September, but most of the field was too wet to carry machinery. Many farmers lost all their wheat that year: we would have lost most of ours except for industry born of desperation. Edmund and I scythed the last and wettest two acres, and my mother helped to tie the sheaves. We dragged the sheaves by hand to higher ground, where we could take a trailer without being bogged. Two acres doesn't sound a lot, but it seemed like a whole farm that year.

It had been assumed by most people that I would be selling up. I was determined not to do so. It was an uphill battle. At the time of my father's death I had six horses and six bullocks. I had also paid a deposit on a thirteen-acre field. I knew I would be expected to sell these animals, my working capital, to pay the debts, so I hid them in the field (it wasn't generally known I was buying it). I sold most of my father's livestock, but was still in debt. One of the three farm men, John, retired. I saved his wages but had less time than before to buy horses, my only hope of recovery.

Let it clearly be understood that I am not a feminist. Some ideas advanced by women's libbers were no more than common sense and don't rightly count as feminism; others would result in women giving up more important rights than equal pay: the right to consideration, to being put first and even to tenderness, which I have heard described by an early bra-burner as 'patronizing'.

My encounters with male chauvinists at that time, though, did bring out some feminist feelings. The bank manager, a reasonable man when I'd done my father's business with him, turned into someone quite different. His determination not to allow me to borrow was hidden in a sort of little-woman-speak. 'Now we can't have you bothering your head with that sort of thing,' he said when I asked for an overdraft. 'Why don't you get married? Then there wouldn't be a problem.'

Almost choking with anger, I managed to ask, 'Had you anyone in mind?'

My sarcasm was wasted. 'Not offhand,' replied the bank manager, 'but I could make some enquiries.' Words, luckily, failed me. I charged out of the bank and went home in a rage.

The little-woman approach seemed most inappropriate in my case. I was big, strong and reasonably intelligent. I'd been selling horses to various police forces and to the Household Cavalry for several years, and had kept myself with the results. I had a two-week holiday every year, owned a reliable car and was paying for my field out of profit. I didn't want to sell my cattle before they were ready, but I had to. That was when I abandoned my cheque book and began to deal entirely in cash. I would sell a broken horse and buy a young one for half the price, plus a couple of cattle. Or I would sell two big bullocks and buy three small ones or six weanlings. The bank manager knew how many cattle I owned, he thought, and often sent someone to check. Nobody ever noticed that I was showing them yearlings; that the bullocks I'd started with were growing younger instead of older. In this way I increased the cattle population from fifteen to seventy-five without spending anything but time. I also increased the shifting population of horses to thirty or so.

*

Even when I had my own tractor, a new one which cost £660, my troubles weren't over. This was to some extent my own fault, patience never having been one of my noticeable virtues.

My father having died, I had cut the workforce from three to two and sold twelve bullocks in order to buy that tractor. But I was still the only driver on the place for the whole of that summer. In haytime, I did my best to combine two roles. I would go to one of the haytime fairs (Kilrush, Spancilhill, Cahirmee and Limerick), setting off at

[65]

some unsocial hour, and buy a horse or two. I would arrange for their transport by train or lorry and try to chase up contacts to secure further deals. This would take all morning and sometimes all afternoon as well. I would dash home, get the tractor out and cut a field of hay.

I won't forget the day of Kilrush fair, June 10th, a Saturday. I had some early hay, a heavy crop which looked as if it might be hard to save if the weather broke. I was at the fair, ninety miles from home, at 8.30 a.m., and bought two horses. When I got home, it was late afternoon and I decided to cut as much hay as I could before dark. It would be ready to turn on Monday. Cutting was slow, as I was still using the old horse-drawn mower, trailing behind the tractor. There was no way of putting it out of gear, so I had to swing round in a circle at the end of every swath. This meant that I was always clogging up the blade with already mown hay and having to disentangle it.

I was nearing the middle of the field – and the end of my task – around 10.30 p.m. There was a square left to cut no bigger than a large room. I was tearing round to finish it when, with a long whoosh, the air went out of one of the big back tyres. Six rounds left to cut. Saturday night. There was nothing to be done, and the field was at the extreme end of the farm, down by the river.

I jumped off the tractor in a fine rage and kicked the flat wheel as hard as I could. I was wearing sandals and I dislocated my big toe. I had to hop all the way home to my mother, who yanked the toe back into place at once. The pain was astonishing but I hardly had time to feel it before the joint snapped back into position.

My mother was in almost as bad a temper as I was, because the horses had arrived from Kilrush while I was gone, and she didn't know where I was. She was seventy and not in the best of health at the time. When the lorry arrived, she had asked the driver to unload the horses and turn them loose into a stable. He asked her to help. She protested, 'Why don't you unload them yourself?'

'I have only one arm,' said the driver. She looked and saw that he had an empty sleeve pinned to his chest like Nelson's; no artificial limb, no stump. Yet this man went to all the fairs with his lorry and took unbroken colts all over the midlands, the south and the west. How he managed to turn his vehicle and back it into awkward places without power steering, I don't know, but he did manage. My mother was so impressed that she agreed to hold one of the horses for him, but when I hopped home I got a less than sympathetic reception.

*

My poor mother – she had a lot to put up with. She must have been bored and lonely, and I was hardly ever in the house. This was a shame, as she was the warmest-hearted and wittiest person I have ever known. Things improved for her when I got married and didn't have to work on the farm.

One of the harder things she had to bear was my taste in music. Mothers of a later generation had to endure all the varieties of pop and rock. Mine had to put up with Irish traditional music, to which I was addicted. It's interesting that it's popular again today.

From an early age, I sensed an association between horses and music. This may have been because Paddy used to sing 'The Rose of Mooncoin' as he ploughed, and a poignant ballad called 'The Night that Alice Died'. (She fell upon the cold, cold ground and never more did rise.) He sang this when he was happy, saying that it encouraged the horses. Perhaps it did.

I used to visit a neighbour's house where different members of the family played the fiddle, tin whistle and button accordion. We sang loudly, and danced until we knocked sparks out of the flagstones. Often we invented ditties about anything that was happening, making them up as we went along. Then television arrived and singing gave way to watching.

Many musicians deserved better instruments. The traditional bodhrán, made of a goatskin and played with a bone, could be made locally; but I have seen fiddles made from butter-boxes and accordions with half the keys missing in the hands of real musicians.

County Clare was and is the place for traditional music, and I'll always remember a day I spent horse-hunting there. I went first to a farmer whose house was so close to the sea as to be almost in it (the door handle was tied to the nearest tree with rope to keep it shut). I bought one horse there and another in Kildysart, not far away, several hours later. In the meantime, I'd visited half a dozen other farms, buying nothing, but collecting hangers-on who wanted to help. In Kildysart, we were invited in for tea and there was quite a crowd. A sing-song started, but nobody had a musical instrument, so we adjourned to the house of the renowned musician, Mrs Crotty. There were several Crottys there and the kitchen was filled to bursting.

It had been raining all day, and we all had wet overcoats and heavy boots. I don't remember any alcohol being around, but I have never drunk so much tea, before or since. We danced too, as well as the cramped space would allow.

After some time, awash with tea, we piled into two cars – there were seven in my Morris Minor – and went to see an old man who was said to be very ill. The idea was to cheer him up, but I was afraid we might be the cause of his death. Not at all. The old man jumped out of his sickbed and joined the party. This was in Kilfenora, so I was gradually heading in the direction of home. At last we said goodbye. I left my companions to find their way home and set off in the dark. Near Corofin, I had a puncture.

It was still raining hard, and no lights were to be seen. At last I flagged down a car driven by a young man and asked if he could help. 'Of course,' he said, 'I'll lend you a flashlamp.' He handed it through the window, adding, 'Leave it on the wall when you've finished with it.' He waved cheerfully as he drove away. I changed the wheel and drove as far as Killaloe where I had another flat. There I had to borrow a wheel, but at least I didn't have to change it.

As before, my mother was alone and worried. Two of my musical friends had decided to deliver the horses with their trailer. This wasn't in the contract so it was a nice surprise for me.

'She left an hour before we did,' said Mike, who owned the trailer. 'I wonder where she got to.'

'I don't know in the face of God,' said Pajoe gloomily. My mother, more worried than ever, asked them in for tea. When I arrived, Mike and Pajoe were trying to cheer her up by singing to her. They chose

Paddy's favourite, 'The Night that Alice Died'. There was relief all round when I appeared and my mother made another pot of tea. Then I fetched my accordion, and the party broke up around 1 a.m.

It was one of those occasions when I had serious doubts about whether the day's work would pay. As it happened, the two horses made plenty of profit. In my book they have been given the names Teaparty and Singalong.

*

At that time, trailers were getting commoner and trains fewer and less convenient. I no longer bicycled to the station in the morning, or rode my purchases home from the station at night, riding the quietest, while the others ran loose and Paddy or Edmund brought up the rear on my bike. No wonder the children of Nenagh used to run alongside shouting, 'Ride him cowboy!' and 'Where are you camping tonight?'

The railways were geared for horses in the fifties. The Dublin Express waited in Nenagh for ten minutes while the blacksmith tacked a shoe on an equine passenger, and I don't remember complaints. I'd remember if there'd been any – it was my horse. Horses travelled slowly, cheaply and uninsured by goods train, or in comparative speed and comfort by passenger train. This could still mean a cattle wagon, but it was hitched to the express and loaded and unloaded at the platform amid the passengers.

One such load became involved with a wedding party in North Cork. The party, large, noisy and happy, was gathered round the bridegroom who was trying to lift his bride into the carriage. She, a sturdy young woman, was about double his weight. 'She's stuck to the ground, lads,' cried the bridegroom, hauling away. Just then, two young horses plunged through the crowd, whinnying and with halters trailing. The bride screamed, the bridegroom abandoned her and jumped into the train, the crowd scattered. The owner of the horses wandered up and took them from a porter who had caught them outside the ticket office. 'Tis ridiculous crowding up the platform with people that don't be travelling,' he said. 'Why the hell didn't they stay in the hotel?'

I was thought wildly lucky to live within five miles of a railway station, and one, moreover, where trains stopped several times a day. In North Cork, the fair-day train ran once a month, so it didn't do to miss it. On my first trip to the area, I bought a horse near Kanturk, and rang up the station to inquire when the train went. 'It's gone. You've missed it. It went yesterday.'

'Yes, but the next?'

'It goes next Thursday three weeks.'

This was trouble indeed. I was a 130 miles from home and the transport of one horse, even if I could hire a lorry, would cancel out the profit I hoped to make, and more. I asked around and heard of a man who owned a trailer and might be found in a pub in a village not far away. I searched him out. 'Could you take a horse to Nenagh?' I asked him.

'I don't travel to remote places,' he replied. His village had better be nameless, but I hadn't heard of it before and it wasn't marked on the map.

There was another man in the pub, listening to our conversation. 'This horse of yours,' he said, 'is it alive?'

'Of course it's alive,' I said indignantly.

'I just have a van,' he said sadly, 'I couldn't carry a horse unless it was cut up.' So I retraced my steps to Newmarket, Co. Cork, where a cattle fair was just ending. My relief was great when I spotted Dan Grey, a cattle dealer from my own town, with a lorry. He agreed to bring the horse home for me, but not for 'a few hours'. So I had to go home without my horse and it turned up the next morning, sharing the lorry with a cow. I bought the cow as well, and I have to admit, she was the luckier purchase of the two.

After my first experience travelling with Marigold, I avoided the railway horse-boxes if possible. Uncomfortable for horse and owner alike, they were also thickly coated with coaldust.

Before the days of fast food, travelling by rail with a horse was a hungry business. One carried sandwiches (ham and coaldust), or chocolate (fruit, nut and coaldust). A resourceful dealer had an aunt who lived in Portlaoise. As the train drew into the station, she appeared with a plate of unpolluted cold beef, which she passed through the window, complete with knife and fork. When he'd finished eating, crossing the Curragh, I think, the ungrateful nephew threw Auntie's knife, fork and china plate out of the window. And they say littering is a recent phenomenon.

CHAPTER TEN

Learning through the Pocket

My early experiences of buying and selling horses taught me a number of valuable lessons. I used to think I'd do better and get on faster if I had some ready cash, and perhaps I would have done. But giving a beginner all the money he needs isn't necessarily doing him a favour. It may be the reverse.

When I started dealing, I had to sell in order to buy. I had to make profit in order to increase my stock. There's an old Yorkshire saying, 'There's only one way to learn – through your pocket', and I've seen it proved correct over and over again. During my time with horses, I met newcomers to the business every year. Some lasted; some didn't. The ones with most to spend often sank without a trace after a short time, while the less well-to-do, obliged to trade with circumspection, survived and prospered. I learned to distrust dealers who boasted of the high prices they had given and the big profits they had made. As in other professions, the most capable don't boast at all.

These big spenders, known as 'highflyers', were regarded with annoyance because they upset the trade, but they didn't last long. One old dealer, speaking of a newly fledged highflyer, put the matter in a nutshell: 'If he's spending his own money, he'll soon break,' he said. 'And he'll soon lose his job if he's spending somebody else's. Either way, we'll be rid of the sod.' We were.

I sold my horses off the land as soon as I'd established some contacts. Apart from the temptation to take a bad price and go home, I had no car and was at the mercy of the weather. Standing in a fair-green on a wet November afternoon waiting for a customer must be one of the most depressing ways of trying to make money known to man.

I was just twenty when I last showed a horse in a fair. He was a prizewinner in the show-ring, a soft, flashy, chestnut four-year-old called Kingfisher. He was handsome enough, and mannerly, but I'd been trying for weeks to teach him to jump, using a low gate with wide bars which most horses treated with respect. Kingfisher would jump at it, rather than over it, knocking it flat every time. At last he smashed it. I was sitting on his back, swearing; Kingfisher was sliding about on the remains of the planks. Two of them were hung round his neck. 'What are you doing?' asked my father, who had a habit of appearing when least wanted or expected.

'Teaching this brute to jump,' I said savagely.

'It looks more as if you were teaching him to ski,' said my father.

It was raining cats and dogs as I rode Kingfisher to Nenagh station to catch the train for Limerick fair. The weather was so awful that, instead of my usual headscarf, I wore an old felt hat of my father's, a hunting mac, heavy corduroy working trousers and laced boots. Rubber riding-boots hadn't yet appeared, and I never rode in gumboots. Obviously, I had no way of carrying a change of clothes.

The fair was almost rained off. Groups of shivering horses cowered in the lee of the walls with their shivering owners. However, it was my lucky day. I'd hardly arrived when I met Gerry Burke, who was then master of the County Clare Harriers. The deal was £100 and £15 for luck. The horse was paying me well (though not as well as he paid Gerry later on), and in payment I got a £100 note. I had never seen one before. The old Irish notes got progressively larger in size as well as in denomination, and the £100 specimen was huge. Delighted, I searched all my pockets for the £15 luck, making up the last of it with threepenny bits and pennies.

A whole £100. I decided against trying to buy another horse in the downpour and headed for the shops. First I tried in two large stores to get my note changed, but without success, so I thought it would be easier if I'd bought something. I would buy an evening dress for the Hunt Ball. I saw just the one I wanted in Todd's window (parchment satin with a halter neck, if anyone is interested). It was marked 'Newest mode, £11'. It was my size, but in my filthy, dripping state, I couldn't try it on, and the assistant looked at me queerly, I thought. Neither would she change the £100 note. So I went to Cruise's Hotel to wash. Only the euphoria caused by the note had prevented me from taking this obvious step first.

I got more curious looks as I tramped, with squelching boots, into the 'Ladies', but it would have taken more than curious looks to dampen my spirits that day. I removed my father's hat and saw, to my dismay, that the dye in the sweatband had run, and there was a broad ginger band across my forehead, with ginger rivulets trickling down my face. No wonder the shop assistant had stared. I scrubbed and scrubbed, and at last got the mark off, wrung out my hair, jammed the hat into my pocket and went to the dining-room where I ordered what was called a 'full lunch', price 3/6.

I enjoyed my meal, and if I steamed as I sat by the radiator, well, I wasn't the only one. When I'd finished, I offered the waiter the £100 note. He wouldn't or couldn't take it and I'd eaten the lunch, so an interesting situation arose. I argued. So did he.

That day, Limerick was full of dud fivers. These were crude copies of the old white and grey English notes called 'flimsies' by some and 'sweetpapers' by others. The children of Limerick were having great fun dropping them in the street and watching people scramble for them. Early in the day, some of them had been passed off successfully; some may have found their way into Cruise's till. Evidently, the waiter suspected my note, which was soggy and dog-eared by this time.

When I had convinced him that I hadn't any more money on me (he found that suspicious too), he carried the note off to the back regions, by one corner at arm's length. He was gone for some time. Eventually, he returned with £99/16/6.

I bought the evening dress and asked for it to be posted home. Feeling on top of the world, I went back to the fair and bought an unbroken three-year-old. I'd forgotten for the moment that I'd ridden Kingfisher to the station, so I'd have to lead it home that night. That was the day that a number of hardy souls, finding they'd taken their horses to the wrong railway station, took a short-cut across the lines and along the tracks to avoid riding all the way round to Carey's Road.

I got someone with a car to take my saddle back, while I travelled on the train with my new filly. I led her home, five miles, in the dark and she resisted all the way. It was still raining like anything.

In the morning, I wondered if I'd got the wrong horse. The filly which, soaking wet, had appeared to be brown, had dried off and turned out to be dark chestnut.

*

My beginner's luck tided me over some sticky patches until I'd a little more scope for making mistakes without ruin.

My first mistake, not as expensive as it might have been, was buying a drugged horse at Limerick fair. I don't count Marigold – she was a nut case, but there was no deception in her sale to me. My drugged horse was by Prophet's Thumb and he too had the thumb mark. I bought Prophetic in spite of an attempt to warn me. People who do this sort of thing are variously described as 'mushes', 'lambs', or 'pigeons'. Pigeons are for plucking until they haven't a feather to fly with. Then they take up some other occupation.

'He thinks you're a lamb,' said the little man in an urgent whisper. 'Run up the ditch while you can.' The little man, a sterling character called Small Paddy, might as well have been talking Chinese. To be called a lamb sounded like a compliment and I hadn't learned about backing out of a deal. Known as backpedalling or running arse-ways up the ditch, it was allowable if the horse had a fault. I couldn't see anything wrong with Prophetic.

He was a big, handsome, coal-black four-year-old, with ears which turned in at the tips. His bit was wrapped in cloth which was quite a usual way to protect the tender corners of a youngster's mouth. He was broken and ridden. The price was moderate. I rode him and he seemed a bit sleepy. This I put down to lack of proper feeding. As I was loading him, Small Paddy sidled up to me and whispered that the rags were soaked in grenadine. 'He'll kill you,' he said. 'A black horse with sorra a white hair will kill seven men.'

'Lucky I'm not a man,' I said. I was young, stupid and sure I could manage anything on four legs. Besides, I daren't have accused the seller in my ignorance and I knew better than to involve Small Paddy. The black horse slouched into the wagon and shut his eyes.

In addition to being a lamb, a pigeon and a mush, I fear I was a flat. The lower level of the horse-dealing fraternity is largely composed, as I daresay is well known, of sharps and flats. Sharps grow fat on the blunders of the flats. Flats buy flatcatchers: showy, useless horses which nobody else will touch. (On a lower level still, I have been warned about sharps and flats in an establishment where I wouldn't have dreamed of staying anyway. I thought my adviser was referring to the human variety just mentioned, but no, there is another meaning. Sharps are fleas, flats are bedbugs. And you thought it was something to do with music, didn't you?)

The next day, I saddled my black horse and spent a lively twenty minutes trying to get onto his back. At last, I managed it by mounting from the right side – that is, the wrong side, if you follow me. No trouble in his slow paces, but as soon as he began to canter he took off and ran away. He didn't quite bolt, I was just able to drag him round the corners of the field. Luckily he tired before I did; I expect he had a hangover.

I got him back to the yard and asked the old gardener to fetch me a double bridle. He was deaf and thought I wanted a double brandy, so he went off to find my father who came out and made maddening comments of the 'Don't say I've never warned you' variety.

It took me six months to teach Prophetic manners, and if I'd been paid by the hour, I'd have earned his value six times over. I didn't cut my losses because he was a super horse. In the end I was able to win a bet by riding him in a musical chairs competition and in bareback jumping, where he won a rosette. I sold him to Tommy Grantham, and he carried the huntsman of the Oakley for many years.

I think it was the incident of the wet day and the £100 note that decided me to buy a car. I could drive the family Ford Prefect, a perfect pig of a car with a perpetually slipping clutch and no appetite for hills, but I was only allowed to use it for shopping. I reckoned up my assets and took the plunge. I sold a bullock and approached the local garage, but it was hard to buy a car that would go, tax it, insure it and ply it with petrol for less than £100. At last I managed it, and the day when I drove it home was a high spot in my life.

This car of mine, a Fiat 500, 1947 vintage, of the type called a Topolino, was a very small car indeed. It cost about half what I get today for a six-weeks-old puppy. It was easy on petrol and was fun to drive, but it had an Italian temperament. Nobody could discover why it sometimes stopped and stayed stopped for hours. Then, for no apparent reason, it would start normally. On good days, it could do 75 m.p.h. downhill with a following wind; on bad days, it just stopped.

The first fair I took it to was Ballinasloe, which starts on Sunday and continues on Monday. An unusual feature of the fair is the church on the hill (it might be more correct to call a horse fair outside a church unusual). The Harvest Festival used to take place that day, and some of the worshippers hastily exchanged hymnbooks for ashplants and plunged into the fair, killing two birds with one stone.

I arrived, proudly driving my car, in time to make a bargain on Sunday afternoon. But although hundreds of horses were dealt for on Sundays, there were always some sellers whose consciences wouldn't allow them to accept any money until next day. My horse's owner was one of these. I could never understand the ethics of this point of view, feeling that the truly virtuous wouldn't go to a horse fair on a Sunday and the others shouldn't be so fussy. He was adamant, so I arranged to return next day, which I did, setting off so as to be there as asked, by 10 o'clock. My car, which had behaved nicely the day before, sighed and died near Laurencetown.

I hitch-hiked the last nine miles and arrived just in time to see the horse being paid for by somebody else. My man had got tired of waiting.

Back home, I complained to the garage-owner that the car was unreliable. 'You bought it at an unreliable price,' he said.

That little car got some rough treatment; I often drove it over terrain more suited to a tractor. Being light, it had the advantage of being easy to push when it broke down. I must have pushed it for miles. I've owned many good cars since then, but I've never known anything to equal the thrill of buying my first. I drove it all over the mountains, seeking bargains, and always freewheeling downhill to save petrol.

One day, I overtook two exceedingly fat and very tall old men. One had a coat, the other hadn't and it was raining hard. The coatless one flagged me down. 'Will you carry us up the mountain?' he asked.

My car had two doors and no back seat. 'I might take one of you,' I said dubiously. So the old boy backed into the seat and sat down, causing my side of the car to leap in the air. His brother, after some struggling and wheezing, lifted his legs in after him and banged the door.

I drove up the hill, and my passenger told me he had a horse to sell, so I took him to the field where it was grazing. I got out and went round to open the door. I couldn't; the extra weight had strained the catch. I fought with it, and at last it flew open, leaving me with the handle in my hand. My troubles were only beginning.

'I'll never get out of this yoke,' said the fat man, 'we'll need the Fire Brigade.' I tried to lift his feet out, but they were wedged. He held out his hands instead. I braced my heels and pulled. He came slowly, head first, halfway through the door. Sundry small objects rained from his pockets. 'Oh God, my blood pressure!' he said, 'Get me out. I'm likely to die if I'm tormented. I could drop any time.'

Feeling callously that I'd rather he didn't die in the car, I dragged at his hands harder than ever, bracing one foot against the wheel. At one point, both offside wheels were clear of the ground. Suddenly, my passenger shot through the door like a champagne cork, the far wheels bounced on the ground and I sat down heavily in the mud.

I'm glad to say, he suffered no ill effects and by the time his brother had arrived on foot, I'd bought the horse. She went to Douglas Bunn and was one of the first to win at Hickstead.

Poor little car, it had a sad end. It let me down once too often and I traded it in with two bullocks and £20 for a Morris Minor, which was slower but surer. The Fiat was sold to Josef Locke, who was on his way to Dublin. I can't imagine why he chose it. Anyway he only got halfway there, and my Topolino lay abandoned on the grass verge near Portlaoise for several years.

CHAPTER ELEVEN

Breakfast the Night Before

I hate Spancilhill fair, one of the oldest horse fairs in Ireland, soaked in tradition. 'Famed in song and story' is the phrase favoured by reporters. There is a song about the place which runs to about half an hour's singing time, according to how long the singer has been in the pub.

My reasons for hating Spancilhill are all personal. I've bought good horses there, but something always went wrong; I'd have done better to stay at home. The fair seemed to be jinxed for me.

Oh yes, the song. I was once obliged to stand in the rain for four hours, holding my Irish draught mare, Brosna Queen, which I was showing in a class. She had no foal and was placid, so I sheltered behind her and waited. Beside me was a man who was less fortunate. His mare perpetually sidled, stamped and fidgeted; her foal, whose halter he held in the other hand, sidled, fidgeted and stamped. It also kept trying to nip him. Nobody volunteered to help either of us and I can't say I'm surprised.

After an hour or two a tinker girl came along, begging. I gave her some loose change and she turned her attention to my companion. She refused (rightly) to believe he had no money on him, and disregarded his objection that he had a horse in each hand. Unwisely, he said, 'If you want any money, you'll have to sing for it.' The girl was charmed with the idea. She stood directly in front of the poor man, about three feet away from him, set her hands on her hips, opened her mouth wide and began to sing 'Spancilhill' at the top of a very loud and raucous voice. Her victim stood it for one verse, then he gave me a horse to hold, plunged a wet hand into his pocket and pulled out a pound note (at least a fiver today). The girl took it, with a beaming smile; but feeling, I suppose, that he should get his money's worth, sang two more verses.

Spancilhill fair is held on midsummer's day. It used to start at first light and go on for a week. The first time I went, I couldn't afford hotel bills, so I asked a dealer when I should start. 'You should leave home by three in the morning,' he said. 'Get your breakfast the night before.' He was right. I overslept, arrived at 6.30 a.m., and found most of the best horses had been sold. I went home horseless after an early breakfast in Ennis.

The reason for the ungodly hour was that most horses travelled by rail, and if they were to catch the English boat, they had to leave Ennis on the morning train.

On my next visit I had my car, and enough cash to stay in the Queen's Hotel in Ennis.

Ireland isn't renowned, even now, for being overdone with sign-posts. They were removed during the war and reappeared gradually in ones and twos. There is one near my home which has been point-ing down the wrong road for more than thirty years. The feeling locally is that anyone who doesn't know the way to Nenagh deserves to get lost. Tourists find out the hard way.

Spancilhill wasn't signposted or marked in any way. If there was no fair on, you could drive straight through it and not realize you'd missed it until you arrived in Ennis. I have a poor sense of direction and on my second visit I had, of course, forgotten the way. Some-where near Tulla, I saw an elderly man building a stone wall by the road. I pulled up and asked politely, 'Could you tell me the way to Spancilhill, please?'

The man paused in his work and considered me, a large stone in his hand. 'I could,' he said at last, and placed the stone in position. He picked up another.

'Aren't you going to tell me the way?' I asked impatiently. He placed the second stone beside the other and stood back to study the effect. 'You might as well be idle as talk to a woman,' he said. Furiously, I drove away, overshot the fair and arrived in Ennis.

In the morning I had no trouble in 'finding' the fair, which stretched for at least a mile in all directions from the crossroad. From time immemorial, it had been a road fair, and although moved to a field nearby in the sixties, it still overflowed in all directions. The lane from the crossroads to the field was narrow, with trailers parked wherever there was room for them, and often where there wasn't. Making one's way along the lane on foot among the milling horses was risky, even for the young and active. The only level place to measure a horse was the main road, and one wasted a lot of time getting there.

The field was bumpy and crowded, but holiday-makers were scarce at 4 a.m. Few of us are at our brightest and best then. Tinkers were everywhere. Men, women, children, horses, ponies, donkeys and goats were all over the place. Galloping a horse was dangerous for everybody. I once saw a horse and rider brought crashing down by a small child leading a greyhound. Child and dog continued on their way, unhurt and unconcerned.

*

My first buy at Spancilhill was a thoroughbred mare called Merry Gold. I couldn't afford her price – £70 – so went halves with a friend. 'You can have the half that eats,' he said. So I bought half a horse for £35, but a couple of weeks later, managed to raise the balance and bought the half that provided valuable manure.

Merry Gold was a good horse and won fourteen point-to-points and a hunter chase. She gave me a shocking fall on the flat when she put her foot in a rabbit hole; we were both lucky to be no more than shaken. This was out hunting, and the country isn't suitable for thoroughbreds unless they are exceptional. There are some great hairy hedges and deep drains full of water. A half-bred horse is usually better at saving itself from awkward situations. There was the story of an angry rider floundering in the mud, shouting to the farmer, 'I thought you said there was a bottom to this drain.'

'There is, but you haven't got down to it yet.'

Lord Huntingdon, who was master of the Ormond Hunt, our neighbouring pack, last century, was known as a reckless rider. He jumped one of these huge, hairy hedges with an unknown amount of deep water beyond, and could be heard splashing and swearing beyond the hedge. A more prudent rider shouted from behind, 'What's on the other side?'

'I am, thank God,' answered his lordship as he galloped away.

Captain Finch, whom I have mentioned before, used to hunt on a little blood mare called Georgina. She came to grief at one of these big drains and fetched up at the bottom of it with the captain underneath. Two farmers arrived with ropes to rescue them and Captain Finch, who was not known for being open-handed, offered them half a crown to pull the horse off him. They wanted ten shillings. A long hard deal then took place, with Captain Finch sitting in the ditch, the horse sitting on Captain Finch and the wreckers bargaining over the price. When it became plain that the old man was prepared to freeze or drown rather than give in, they agreed on five shillings and pulled the horse clear without more ado.

Captain Finch was a great one for hunt balls and never missed a dance. Whatever the tune, whatever the rhythm, he danced a Viennese waltz at double speed, with spin turns, while shouting at the fox-trotters, the quick-steppers and the smoochers in corners to get out of his way. 'Don't you know any other dances?' asked my mother, almost too dizzy to stand.

'There *are* no other dances,' was the reply.

There is an ancient legend about the ruin of Castletroy, a few miles from Limerick. The castle, it is said, will never fall until the handsomest man in Ireland passes beneath it. Then down it will come and squash him flat. Captain Finch had been a handsome man in his day. His vanity was such that, when driving past Castletroy, he always crossed the road, so as to be out of range of the falling masonry. When he was about seventy he decided, in the interests of safety to the general public, to go to Limerick only by train.

I had some eccentric relations myself. One, a keen racing man towards the end of last century, lived in England and attended every major race meeting. He was a great betting man and lucky with it.

At a dinner party, shortly before the Derby of 1895, he swore in front of witnesses that he would name his unborn child after the winner of the big race. The baby was due on Derby day. His wife was appalled. 'Supposing it's a girl?' she said.

Her husband was used to getting his own way. 'It won't be a girl,' he stated.

On the eve of the race, the lady gave birth to a daughter. In vain, she pleaded that the winner of the Oaks might have a name more suitable for a baby girl. Fortunately for her, she was ignored. The Oaks was won by Lonely. The midwife was somewhat taken aback by her patient's anxiety to hear news of the ante-post betting on the Derby. As it happened, she liked a bet herself and was able to provide the information that Paradox was favourite. 'My husband doesn't think he'll stay,' she said. 'He fancies Red Ruin and he's backed the winner three years running.'

At these words, the poor lady is said to have fainted away. However, fate was reasonably kind, Melton won the Derby and the child was christened Melton Vera. If there had been television in 1885, little Melton's mother would have had some tense moments. Xaintrailles led the field at Tattenham Corner, with Red Ruin and Paradox just behind. It was only Fred Archer's jockeyship that landed Melton home after a tremendous struggle in the last 150 yards.

Life is a drabber business now that there are fewer real eccentrics about. There may be some left, but signs of eccentricity are probably dealt with by long-term medication and, of course, counselling. I can't think of a single character who summons his family to meals with a hunting horn, or persists in going in and out by a window in preference to the front door. I knew a man who always went in and out by the window because it was easier to open and shut. His visitors were allowed to use the door, if they were tactless enough to insist.

Perhaps the oddities of such people have been directed into useful channels. Anyone who wants to be buried alive for a week or two, or live at the top of a tree, can find sponsors and give the money to charity. Or a newspaper will give him money to write about his experiences – if you can call them that. His behaviour is still, in the eyes of most, abnormal, but it is acceptable.

One real eccentric, who gave me some trouble, was a dedicated woman-hater. He had a good horse to sell, and I had asked a farmer in that area to look out for horses for me. I went to see it and the farmer took me along, telling me that the owner was sick in bed and couldn't see me that day. He then admitted that Benjamin, the owner, spent all his time in bed and had a violent aversion to women. I reluctantly agreed to deal through a third party.

This took place more than a hundred miles from my home. In due course I got word to go and collect my horse, and my go-between met me in the village. I'd previously sent on a cheque and, as we loaded the horse into my trailer I asked if the woman-hater had made a fuss.

'No, I let on you were a man.'

'There can't be many men called Marjorie,' I remarked.

As it happened, Benjamin had realized that he'd been tricked and had thrown the cheque into the fire. My poor go-between got into terrible trouble and wasn't allowed to do any more deals for Benjamin.

*

One of my first horse-fair memories is of a fight between two men, aged perhaps sixty. Were they alive today, I expect they'd be annoyed to feature in a chapter largely about eccentrics. This was no vulgar roughhouse, it was more like a duel. I was riding a horse, so had a grandstand view of the proceedings.

I don't know what they quarrelled about. They weren't drunk; they didn't shout. They had seconds. Each was wearing a long black overcoat and these they handed to their seconds. They then set about each other with sticks, in grim silence.

A crowd gathered, cheering and urging them on. Both combatants wore hats and, judging by the yells of their supporters, a knocked-off hat would mean either victory or a win on points. I have never seen anything like it, before or since – elderly men settling their differences with ashplants. What stuck in my mind was their respectable appearance and their lack of visible emotion. Both hats were knocked off and the seconds stepped in but were shaken off impatiently. The fight continued until one of the combatants got a crack on the head which felled him.

The winner, panting slightly, put on his overcoat and his hat. The loser was helped to his feet and the two shook hands.

'What was that about?' I asked someone in the audience.

'Ah, they were passing the time. Old men have no sense.'

Violence of the sort common in the cities today was notably absent from the fairs, except for the odd pub fight. Violent incidents usually occurred when somebody had misbehaved and was summarily dealt with. On my first trip to the monthly fair at Clonmel, I saw two men throw a third into the river. They handled him as casually as if he'd been a sack of rubbish and walked away, talking together. The other man climbed out of the river without much bother and hurried off, with nervous backward glances. I never heard why such rough justice was called for, and nobody took any further notice of the victim.

*

When I went to my first fair, I had no money to spend, so I spent my time watching those who had, and listening. It was 1948, there was no European trade except for horses for slaughter. But thousands of army and police horses were still being exported. Most went to England, quite a large number to Canada. I watched and asked questions and bided my time.

The cheapest horses being bought for army work were the 'gunners'. They were bays, and at that time, chestnuts too, on the heavy side for riding, smallish and active. The officers' chargers were chestnut or grey, and of high-class hunter type.

'If I could just pick up one or two trumpeters, we could go home,' said a red-haired man in Kilrush. Another eccentric? No, this was the well-known shipper Dick Morgan, to whom I would sell many a horse in time to come. He was looking for trumpeters' horses for the mounted band of the Household Cavalry. They would be light, or dappled grey geldings, about 15.3 hands and not easily upset.

The kettledrums are carried by vast skewbald carthorses, and every dealer in Ireland was constantly looking out for one. The biggest demand was for blacks for the Household Cavalry, which came in two sorts, 'troopers' and 'riders'. The troopers were a mixed lot. You could get a real common sort accepted if he had a small head and light action. A much better stamp of horse would fail if he had a slack back, sloppy action or carried his head badly. I never bought a black trooper unless certain I could pass him on. They had no other job.

Right up to the eighties, all the Household Cavalry horses came from Ireland. There were experiments with horses imported from Germany and Hungary around then, but I don't think they amounted to much. The move away from Irish horses may have started in 1982, after the IRA bomb in London which killed seven horses. The bond between the English buyers and the Irish dealers who supplied them was very strong, and I remember the horror and revulsion we all felt at the time. There was a whip-round, and enough money was raised to replace the horses, which would then have cost from £400 to £700 each off the land.

When horses were plentiful and cheap, there was still nice profit to be made from buying 'lifeguards'. Mares were bought at the same rate as geldings, although we bought them off the farms much more cheaply. They were allowed some white on the legs, but no more than a star on the face. As blacks became scarce, these rules were relaxed and white blazes allowed.

The agents who showed the lifeguards to the British army buyers clipped them all over, whatever the time of year. This helped to sell the commoners, but made the rejects unmistakable when they appeared in the next fair.

By far the biggest buyers of blacks were the O'Donnell brothers from Buttevant, Co. Cork. They were at every fair and had agents buying for them all over the country. I can remember hundreds of their horses running loose in Doneraile Park. I would try to corner some of them on a bridge with two gates across it; not the best place to buy anything.

Before my time the O'Donnells had a huge army trade, selling both to the British and to the Germans on the eve of the Second World War. The British colonel wasn't too pleased when he discovered who the customers in the kitchen were. He had to comfort himself with the fact that he had been entertained in the parlour.

When the last boatload of horses sailed from Waterford, just as war broke out, the O'Donnells had a consignment of several hundred horses on its way to Waterford. They were stopped at the town of Tallow on the Cork/Waterford border. There they grazed the long acre while the brothers sent out word that there were good cheap horses to be bought on the Tallow Road. That was the origin of the Tallow Road fair which was held there ever after, early in September.

Sometimes at a fair, word would go round: 'The army's been.' That meant that any black for sale, or anything clipped out in the summer, was a reject. I stuck to 'riders' (officers' charger types which weren't usually clipped), and bought a lot of cheap blacks in this way, after making sure they hadn't been turned down for unsoundness. A horse with too much white or not up to enough weight wouldn't be shown again and could be bought cheaply as a hunter. My 'rejects' also included a good showjumper called Big Brother and a show-horse called Halifax.

*

One time when I thought there would be some ready-made troopers about was when a firm of Limerick undertakers changed from horse-drawn to motorized hearses. I got wind of this and went to see if I could buy some blacks cheap. White markings weren't accepted then, but I knew that the hearse horses were all as black as ink. The undertaker explained that the horses were on the elderly side. He was right, they were a moth-eaten lot. There was only one young one, he said, a four-year-old, and he'd gone to the guards. I thought he meant the Lifeguards, but he explained that the Garda sergeant in the local police barracks had bought the horse – and might well take profit. So

I went to the barracks to find out. The sergeant wasn't around, and the constable on duty seemed disinclined to let me see the horse. There was a long telephone discussion and at last he said, 'Okay, you can see the horse, but I can't get it out.'

Bewildered, I followed him along a passage to a cell. It was the overnight lock-up for the drunk and disorderly and, in those more law-abiding days, it was seldom needed. On this occasion it was occupied by a big, strapping black gelding. He didn't just occupy the cell; he almost filled it. He was well bedded up with straw, and the constable pointed out the convenient washbasin which could be filled with oats or water. There was a full hay-net tied to the central bar of the little window, and the big black could hardly have looked cosier.

This horse was too heavy for me to buy. I couldn't risk being left with him, but I returned with another dealer who bought him after he'd been released with a foot-long key and brought out of doors. This dealer had flatly refused to believe that the horse was being kept in the cells.

*

In this part of Ireland, a stable is usually called a house. English people, hearing that the horse was 'in the house', half expected to find it in the kitchen. I never saw as unusual a stable as the police cell, but I once bought two horses out of a real house. The owner had got married and built a new bungalow. The horses were in a room in the old house with paper on the walls, a marble fireplace and a door with a brass knocker.

Another time, I bought a horse which was eating silage at a barrier with a herd of bullocks. The bullocks were getting the lion's share and it took weeks to get the horse clean. Another of my purchases was having silage forked out to him in a field. He was the fattest horse I ever bought. 'Shaking with meat,' said his owner. I knew the man well, so I took the horse on trust as I daren't have galloped him for his wind. On grass, Pilgrim, as he was called, lost weight at an alarming rate. It took the whole summer to get him right and I never again bought one which had been fattened on silage.

Another colt I bought was sharing his living-quarters with four calves. He also shared their skimmed milk, hay and roots. He had a wonderful shine on him, but the calves had eaten his tail and it never grew properly. A funny thing about him was that having lived with calves he'd caught some of their ways. He always lay down when not actually eating, and he used to turn his head and lick his sides. All cattle do this, there's something wrong if they don't, but I've never known another horse to do it.

While a stable is often called a 'house' in Tipperary, it is more often a 'cabin' in County Clare. On the windswept, marshy acres of West Clare, most farmers looked after their horses well. Even in March, at Kilrush fair, you could see one young horse after another arriving, bright-eyed and satin-skinned, obviously having been well cared for.

They had cost a lot to keep all winter, but they made top prices, especially for army and police work. The stables, or cabins, where they lived were usually pretty small, having doors more suited to donkeys. A sort of deep-litter system was used, so the horse was getting near the roof by springtime. The owner would open the door, revealing a set of legs and the lower half of a horse's body. He would go inside and presently emerge, holding the end of a rope and making encouraging noises. Then the horse would lower its head, bend its knees and follow him.

If these youngsters hadn't been kindly handled and properly fed, getting them out would have been a major operation. As it was, they crept in and out of their cabins without any fuss. If I wanted a young horse to go hunting on, I always tried to get one which had been bred and reared in West Clare. The land elsewhere in Ireland is far better, but where the cow was queen, young horses had to make do with the leavings. Often their constitutions were undermined by neglect and poor feeding.

CHAPTER TWELVE

Fundraising

I have often been accused of selling the horse from under me, but this is only partly correct. My hunter was generally for sale, but I was usually supposed to be whipping in, and felt obliged at least to finish the day. In one year, 1954 I think, I rode eleven different horses without a fall, whipping in off most of them.

A friend of mine sold the horse from under him at the opening meet to a dealer who liked its looks. This animal was known as 'The Churn', because of the obscene noises it made when it trotted. It was handed over at once.

The hunt was noted for frequent changes of mastership and, more often than not, it was run by a committee with a kennel huntsman and an acting master. Our committee meetings sometimes went on into the small hours. The meetings were held in a lounge bar; regular patrons had to drink elsewhere. Often, tempers were lost. I remember once, a violent argument broke out and, one by one, the committee members resigned. One by one, we retired to the saloon bar to discuss the matter in depth. When everyone had resigned except the instigator of the argument, he went home. We re-elected ourselves, returned to the lounge and wound up the meeting. We broke up, the best of friends, around 2 a.m.

I was secretary for three years and it was a terrible job. Another secretary entered the following in the minute book: 'The committee's decision was not to decide what to decide until a decision had been reached.'

Our various masters liked to sell their horses to augment their guarantees, and I was often asked for the loan of one of mine for the huntsman who had just sold his own. One of our dealing masters arrived at a meet in full hunting regalia, riding a bicycle. 'Why the bike?' asked the field-master.

'Because I couldn't sell it,' was the reply.

These huntsmen rode some funny horses at times. The animals provided by the committee had one thing in common: they were cheap. They had to be. They could jump, even if their looks and breeding left much to be desired. They would, as the saying went, go a long way in a long time.

When huntsmen provided their own horses, the problem was even greater as they were liable, like the bicycling master, to sell them on the way to the meet. I have had my own horse hijacked by a huntsman whose own old veteran had given up. Another put his whip up on a horse which had, he said, been saved from the boiler. This animal didn't live on borrowed time for long. His heart gave out in mid-air as he was jumping a wall and he dropped like a brick.

This was just before Ballinasloe fair and I was having a look round for hunters in that area. I was directed to the house of a man called Peter, who had a four-year-old in the paddock with the longest mane I have ever seen. Peter bridled the colt, thrust his foot into the mane and, using it as a stirrup, mounted. Two locks of hair had been knotted together for the purpose. I asked the price. Peter told me. I didn't bid him as I'd been told he was subject to fits and I didn't want to bid half the asking price until he was on the ground. I could hardly ask him to dismount in case he had a fit when he heard my offer, so I had to go away.

A few weeks later, I recognized Peter's horse, shorn of most of his mane, carrying the huntsman. Peter had had a fit, I was told, but was recovering.

*

My hunting being confined to North Tipperary, with brief visits to Galway and Limerick, I was constantly told that things were very different in England. Spit and polish, tradition gloriously upheld – it didn't sound too cheerful. The North Tipperary Hunt was then notably lacking in spit and polish.

Yet, when I went out on foot with an English pack run by farmers in Yorkshire, it was remarkably like home. A fierce argument broke out at the meet over the sale of a horse, my host wore a felt hat and wellies, the hunt terrier had a bloody fight with a pet dog a lady had brought with her on a lead, there was talk of barley and silage. Just like home.

Our only concession to Tradition with a capital T was our field-master, the later Peter Anderton, a man who was a stickler for etiquette, sadly out of place in North Tipperary. He would lecture the children at the meets (who didn't listen, anyway). 'You must treat the master with due respect at all times,' he said. 'Remember he comes second only to God.'

> In the year of Our Lord, twenty-seven,
> I used to go out with the Quorn.
> I knew I was nearer to Heaven
> Than those who were lowlier born.
> For the Master himself once addressed me,
> 'Go to hell, you unprintable sod!'
> His command of the language impressed me
> For I knew he came second to God.
>
> I used to go out with the Cottesmore
> When I was a sub in the Blues –
> I was owing my tailor and lottesmore
> And hadn't a whole lot to lose...

I don't remember all of this ditty, but it ended:

> ... A person of breeding and merit,
> A credit to good mastership,
> He sleeps with four dogs and a ferret
> While his wife goes to bed with the whip.

And now that the matter is reckoned,
I've come to the end of my song –
Put God first and your MFH second
And you'll never go very far wrong.

Spit and polish can be carried to extremes. I think this may be a legacy from the days when a high proportion of masters were army officers, and from the traditional connection between hunting field and battlefield.

There was and, in some places still is, a belief that an army or ex-army man is the most suitable person to fill the post of MFH, Pony Club instructor or showing judge. Okay, if the man has hunting or jumping experience, but hard to explain if he is familiar only with tanks. I suppose the idea persists because of the long history of horses in the army, although most had been replaced by armoured vehicles fifty years ago.

It is a fact that many men have joined the army because of a love of horses. I find this hard to understand. Horses have always suffered hideously in war. Some leader observed that you could ride your horse as long as it was mobile, shelter behind it when it was down and eat it when it was dead. Perhaps he was a horse lover, perhaps merely practical.

*

I remember the very first electric fences, obstacles which gave us some unpleasant surprises. My horse, Gilligan, spread one all over my neighbour's field on a day I won't forget. There has always been wire, but you can cope if you can see it. The killer is the rusty strand of barbed wire which you can't, often held up by a thin, sharp stake, leaning at a drunken angle.

When I was very young, I saw a young woman heavily thrown and her horse staked, at just such a deceptive fence. She lay, out for the count, while her horse struggled to his feet with a horrible gash in his side. Luckily, the field included both a doctor and a vet. They gave their horses to me to hold, also the staked horse. I had to hold my own pony as well, so it was difficult, but earned me half a crown. (After that, I tried to be around if anyone needed a vet or a doctor.)

The doctor pulled a first-aid tin out of his pocket and set to work to stitch up the staked horse. The vet rushed to help the young woman (who was very pretty) and lent her his horse to ride home on.

I saw (and felt) my first electric fence several years later. I'd heard about them, of course; they were an interesting novelty, a gimmick. 'They'll never catch on,' we said. This fence was a single strand of steel wire, erected about a horse's length away from a fly fence on the landing side. It was around three feet high and pretty well invisible.

A friend of mine was riding a flighty and not particularly intelligent mare, so at first I took no notice when I was told she was 'playing the fool'. The mare, that is. But she had managed to get astride the wire, with a foreleg and a hindleg on either side. Her yard-high leaps, seen from a field away, puzzled us. What on earth was she doing? Then we saw the wire and unkind laughter was heard.

We regretted the laughter as, by the time the circling hunt was over, most of us had been entangled in that wire. It wouldn't break, packed a hefty punch and was said to be linked directly to the Shannon Scheme.

I don't think the worst falls happen out hunting. Most serious accidents happen on the road and, at the time I'm writing about, our roads were very quiet. But there were still hazards if your horse was young, well bred and excitable. One wet day I was riding a filly called Clarianna to the blacksmith's when we met an old man cycling down the middle of the road. He was wobbling quite a bit, having only one hand on the handlebars. With the other, he held up what used to called a 'priest's umbrella' – a very large, black one. Clarianna almost fainted. She was so frightened that, fortunately, she didn't know which way to jump. She stood perfectly still, with bulging eyes, shaking all over. In cowardly fashion, I dismounted and held her until cyclist and umbrella were out of sight. On my way home, when it had stopped raining, I met the same man, walking. 'You frightened the wits out of my horse,' I told him.

'Sell it,' he said, 'buy something less emotional.'

One reason why horses fall is lack of nerve on the part of their riders. Nerve gets horse and rider over big obstacles. Sad to say, courage is no substitute for nerve. You may fool your nearest and dearest but you won't fool your horse. A 'patent safety' may restore his rider's courage, but not his nerve. The horse senses his rider's hesitation, and hesitation is fatal when jumping.

An elderly man, whose nerve had been well and truly lost years before, hired a quiet horse in order to trot around the roads, watching the hunt from a safe distance. When an angry farmer stopped him and demanded £5 in payment for a five-barred gate 'smashed to ally jiggets by you and your bloody horse', he was so pleased that he paid up at once.

With most packs in England, there is a posse following the hunt, doing running repairs. Trainer Mick Easterby, a man with undoubted nerve, riding a bad racehorse, came across some Middleton Hunt followers, dubiously inspecting a high timber fence. 'I'll smash the top rail for you,' said Mick, 'This bugger has a heart like a duck.' He duly smashed it. I can only imagine what the farmer said.

In this part of the world, people have only recently become accustomed to jumping timber, or the 'stick in the gap'. We used to jump almost anything to avoid timber; the hairiest bank, the boggiest drain. When my husband came hunting here as a visitor, I lent him a three-year-old. He gained a reputation for reckless bravery by jumping a three-foot pole in preference to a six-foot bank with a bog drain either side. He, on the other hand, thought he was being prudent and that we were showing off.

When I visited Yorkshire, I jumped a wide drain in order to avoid a post-and-rails, and was praised for my daring. I smiled modestly, but I daren't have jumped the rails.

*

Hunting in North Tipperary was cheap, and cost me only a nominal subscription, but there was a snag. Along with other supporters, I was much in demand for fundraising activities.

All sorts of difficulties beset the hunt committee, and most of them were to do with finding things. These things included foxes, masters, new subscribers and cash. When, after a long search, a master was found, money had to be raised to pay his guarantee, and I was put in charge of running some dances.

There can hardly be a less profitable event than a hunt dance, described as a 'social' in order to avoid paying entertainment tax. These socials were by invitation only, so they involved a great deal of work, including the making of huge piles of ham sandwiches and handing round of same. The committee of eight rapidly dwindled to three, at which stage we rebelled. The socials were reduced from six to two a year, which was plenty.

The fashionable way to raise money today is by sponsorship, but that hadn't been thought of at the time. You can find sponsors for almost any activity now. Hunt personnel try to persuade each other to sponsor their children to ride somewhere at so much a mile. Of course, if you can interest the media, you might find someone willing to sponsor you to ride from Cork to Belfast on a donkey or in a pram. This is true dedication.

Another time-honoured way of making money is the raffle or draw. Selling tickets is a poor way of making friends – in fact you lose the friends you already have. It is probably the most reliable way of raising cash, provided that enough thick-skinned ticket-sellers can be found.

I organized a raffle for a pony once. Members felt that it wouldn't pay, and I was allowed hunt funds to buy it only on condition that I guaranteed to sell enough tickets to cover the outlay. This took less than a week. One of the other prizes was a sheepdog puppy. I had to promise this before it was born, but disaster, it died at a week old. This meant that I had to ring up other breeders until I found a replacement, and pay for it. Then the business man who won it asked for cash instead. I paid him. Meanwhile, I was trying to find a customer for the puppy. As it wasn't my own breed, my customers preferred to wait for the next litter. The puppy was six months old before I found a home for him. And I'd named him Lucky.

In the interval between the death of my own puppy and the purchase of Lucky, I was trying to sell a ticket to a farmer. He asked about the pup, and I began to say that it had died and I was getting another. He interrupted furiously, before the second part of my sentence, 'I didn't think you were sunk so low that you'd try to sell tickets for a dead dog.'

*

The hunt ball was a much better money-spinner than the old socials, but involved a lot more outlay. The socials were held in a gloomy upstairs hall, where the paper chains were never taken down for reasons of economy. During the more vigorous dances, the floor would shake alarmingly, dislodging flakes of plaster and cobwebs from the ceiling of the room below. We used to wonder seriously if it might give way. As money was our motive, we crammed as many bodies as we could into the room, and it was probably a good thing that the insurance regulations were tightened up. Hunt balls were held in hotels, so were normally downstairs, but even they had un-foreseen risks.

The hunt chairman at one time was a bank official; a rather fussy man who liked things to be just so. He can't have been much more than five feet tall, and was known for his meticulous dress and for his insistence that everybody behave nicely. He and I were an ill-matched pair on the dance floor.

The hunt ball was in the Lakeside Hotel at Killaloe, and the windows opened onto the garden. As we waltzed by the window, the sash was pushed up from outside, and blurred but truculent voices deman-ded entry at half price because the dance was half over.

My partner, courteous as always, bent down to explain politely why this was impossible. He was immediately seized by the collar and dragged half way through the window. I grabbed his coat tails and shouted for help; two men came to our assistance just as the coat began to split at the waist. The secretary and I then caught hold of a leg apiece and hauled the poor gentleman to safety, minus his white tie. After that, the windows were kept bolted.

It is a tradition here to hold the hunt ball on New Year's Eve. One of my earliest memories is of my parents setting off for the ball dressed in white tie and tails (him) and apricot taffeta (her). My nurse said when they'd gone, 'You won't see them again till next year.' Although the feeble joke was soon explained – it was only a few hours to midnight – the feeling of alarm stayed with me for ages.

As I grew older, and the apricot taffeta got shabbier, I used to envy my parents profoundly. I imagined something like the ballroom scene in the first film I ever saw, some Viennese soufflé with Nelson Eddy in it: chandeliers, Champagne, beautiful people, beautiful dresses, an orchestra playing the Blue Danube, romantic moments in the moonlit conservatory.

I asked questions, and discovered that the hunt ball wasn't at all the fairy-tale event I'd imagined. At that time, it took place in an ice-cold upper room in the Courthouse. On one occasion, a lady put her foot through a rotten floorboard, and the hole was still there the following year. The year after that, it had been patched with the lid of a biscuit tin. After one of these events, my parents stayed overnight in an even icier place, a huge, freezing mansion called Traverston. They huddled, shivering in the kitchen, warming their hands in their coat sleeves because the drawing-room fire had gone out.

'What about a nightcap?' said their host. What a brilliant idea! They accepted eagerly, and were rewarded with tepid Ovaltine and stale cream crackers.

About fifteen years later, I inherited my mother's apricot taffeta, and set off for my first ever hunt ball, which was also my first proper dance. I was nineteen, and was odd woman out, having been invited along by a married couple.

There was a dinner party first, where I sat between a stone deaf man of about eighty and a totally silent elderly woman. I was afraid that, if I ate much, my dress would burst, as I was two stone heavier than my mother and ten inches taller. However, I couldn't resist chocolate sauce with my ice-cream, and poured it on with a liberal hand. Alas, it was brown gravy, which should have been removed with the joint.

My companions either didn't notice or pretended not to. In the end, I ate hardly anything, but I split the dress anyway.

Many years afterwards I attended a hunt ball in Limerick where, by an oversight, soup was served at the end of the meal instead of coffee. I'd been having an argument with my partner who was still huffy. When I remarked, 'That's soup, not coffee,' he replied, 'Rubbish.' Mind you, it was the sort of Oxo consommé that isn't unlike black coffee to look at. My partner put a spoonful of sugar in his mug, stirred it and took a generous swallow. I managed not to gloat too much.

One hunt ball which plumbed the depths was held in the Scout's Hall in Nenagh in the early fifties. The band we'd engaged was run by Rinty Monaghan, a boxer, and was unusually expensive. Rinty shadow-boxed while his band performed and they were immensely popular. However, they didn't turn up until 1 a.m. having been engaged for 9.30. In the long, cold interval, a lady played the piano and some of us sang.

When I started going out, dress dances in the country were commonplace. The country-house hunt ball could be wonderful or awful, depending on the band, the host, the finances of the hunt and, above all, the heating. One which I attended took place in a vast house heated only by a few – very few – oil stoves, dotted about in the immense rooms. They were as dangerous as they were inefficient. At another dance, where the catering was by the ladies' committee, the ladies concerned almost came to blows and had to be separated forcibly.

When dress balls gave way to dinner dances, and dinner dances gave way to discos, the old timers made some concessions to changing times, but not many. Our oldest hunting men, who never went to other dances, turned up each year, their scarlet coats reeking of mothballs, dancing away to whatever music the disco had to offer, and doing away with enormous quantities of booze. Anybody who thinks that Molly Keane's marvellous description of a hunt ball in *Good Behaviour* is exaggerated can take it that they're wrong. It's understated if anything.

Hunt balls are perhaps the only social occasions where such snippets of conversation can be heard as, 'How are you off for flesh?' 'The new draft seem a nice, level lot', or 'Her eyes are brighter today, but her legs are still puffy.' This refers of course to the owner's mare, not his wife.

At these functions, respectable citizens may blow hunting horns, whoop, holloa and dance on tables. The odd thing is, that often quite old people are the most childishly happy. Perhaps it's because they go out less often than their children – and grandchildren.

*

'Can you hold them back for another five minutes?' asked an anxious lady, sheltering behind a stack of cardboard boxes.

'We'll do our best,' gasped the two strong men, specially trained for the job. Angry muttering and an occasional yell came from the struggling mob outside the double doors.

No, it wasn't the end of a siege, although the ladies in the village hall were in some physical danger. When the doors burst open on the stroke of three, the customers surged into the hall where a jumble sale in aid of the hunt was being held, back in the fifties.

The crowd descended as one man (or woman) on the stalls where jam and home-made cakes were displayed. These were cleared in seconds, and the buyers converged on the clothes counter. The counters were trestles, wobbly trestles at that. The buyers were so eager, the bargains so good, that they forced the trestles back against the wall. The sellers, including myself, were in some danger of being cut in half. One old man, who never missed a sale, bought all the shirts on offer, regardless of size, price or style. His methods of getting to the front were, I suppose, no less crude than those of many a London commuter in rush hour. He called these events 'jungle sales', a good name for them.

Everything was sold within an hour, and we counted up a heartening amount of money before going home to recover.

The sales have calmed down since then. There are more chain stores offering low-priced goods. It is positively chic to patronize second-hand and swap-shops. Jumble sales are no longer actually dangerous.

Some people who should have known better habitually sent in stuff which should have gone straight into the dustbin. We dumped these offerings out of sight. A friend of mine, a tireless organizer, told me proudly that she had been promised a fur coat for the sale by a well-to-do lady. The coat arrived on the morning of the sale in a large cardboard box. It smelled of camphor and – something else? We lifted it up cautiously, and maggots rained out of it. My friend crammed the coat back into the box and ran, shuddering, with it to the yard behind the hall. There we doused the whole lot with paraffin and burned it.

I priced jumble all morning, but had to be absent from the sale. I called to help clean up when it was over, and met my friend, looking shaken. 'The owner of the coat's just been in,' she said. 'She asked how we'd got on with it.' There was still a powerful reek of paraffin and burning musquash in the area.

'My God. What did you say to her?'

'I told her it was the very first thing to go. Luckily she was in a hurry, she went off all smiles.'

*

One of the reasons I was in demand to sell raffle tickets was that I spent so much time at fairs and marts. There wasn't much money about in the fifties and sixties, but the dairy farmers and cattle dealers had as much as anybody in country areas. More to the point, they loved a gamble and were generous about parting with it. I would take a dozen books of tickets to the big fairs, and sell them in an hour.

My favourite of all the big fairs was the Old Cahirmee fair at Buttevant in County Cork. Now July 12th means different things to different people, but for those who trade in horses, it means Cahirmee fair. Buttevant, on the main road from Limerick to Cork, was a garrison town during British rule. Wherever there were soldiers, horses were needed for a variety of purposes. Not only were re-mounts constantly required, but also large numbers of harness horses. In addition, there was a thriving trade for hunters. The demand for horses locally provided an incentive to breed better-class animals. Buttevant became a centre for breeding and dealing, supplying not only the British army, but armies and police forces all over the world.

County Cork, mainly thanks to Noel C. Duggan, became the centre of the successful move to reclaim the Irish draught, which was almost an endangered species, and the little town of Millstreet has become host to a great international horse show.

Cahirmee was always a favourite of mine, just as Spancilhill was not. In thirty years, I don't think I ever bought an unlucky horse there. The first time I went, I was fresh from the fiasco of arriving at Spancilhill when the fair was over, so I secured a lift and arrived around 6 a.m. This was a mistake on the right side. The fair started about 8 o'clock and the town was impassable by 9. Too bad if you wanted to drive from Limerick to Cork. The fair used to be enlivened by the yells, oaths and hootings of enraged motorists. A traffic diversion by Doneraile was introduced at last, not a minute too soon.

I wandered disconsolately up and down the main street on my first visit to the fair. Nobody was about and I was hungry. This was another 'breakfast the night before' fair I'd assumed, so I'd made sandwiches – and left them on the kitchen table.

I was passing a tobacconist's shop when I was stopped in my tracks by a glorious smell of frying bacon. I walked by the shop twice more before deciding that an inquiry could do no harm. I knocked on the door and an elderly woman opened it and invited me to have breakfast with her and her family. I had eggs and bacon and two cups of tea and, with difficulty, persuaded her to take some money. She told me that, if I was lunching in town, I could buy a steak at the butcher's and she would cook it. This seemed too much of an imposition, so I didn't take her up on it, but went to the hotel.

This was my biggest mistake of the day. Never, in the course of a long career, have I been offered food as vile as that provided by that hotel. 'What is it, boiled dog?' shouted an angry voice.

'No, it's meat,' said the waitress.

I left my washing-up-water soup, my boiled whatever-it-was, my raw potatoes, liquid grey cabbage and melting, onion-flavoured ice cream. Even the tea was undrinkable, resembling liquid brown boot polish. I had to pay three times the price of my breakfast for this lot. Afterwards, a number of people told me I'd been mad to go there. I wished they'd told me sooner.

I never went into the hotel again, so it may have improved drastically. There was no room for disimprovement. In later years, I went to a shop which operated as a café on fair days, providing ham, tomatoes, bread, butter and tea at a modest price. Country-town hotels weren't good at the time, and even the better ones let down their standards with a bang on fair days. They put sawdust on the floors and provided a feed rather than a meal. If you want to know the difference, it is that a feed comes all on one plate, no choice, meat, veg, spuds and half a pint of brown gravy over the top. If anyone says this is a description of a meal, he is wrong. It is a feed.

In case you are wondering why I didn't take a thermos and sandwiches to the fairs, I will quote a very true saying by a man who made his living out of horses for sixty years. 'The job never would stand drinking,' he said. 'When it won't stand eating it'll be time to give over.'

CHAPTER THIRTEEN

The Creamery

It is time I left the horses and returned to the more mundane ways in which I tried to make a living. For I continued to work hard on the farm and to buy and sell cattle. I'd been horse-dealing for almost ten years when my father died, and the two years which followed were extremely stressful. Although I had Paddy and Edmund working on the farm, I had to do the tractoring, as well as buying and selling stock, plus buying as many horses as possible as cheaply as possible, and trying not to neglect my mother too much. My dealings were in cash and I kept my head down.

As I couldn't live on nothing without somebody noticing, I tried to make the cows pay. I'd been separating and churning milk, and selling butter in the shops for years. It was either so plentiful that I couldn't get rid of it or so scarce that there wasn't any going spare to sell. Top price was around 10p a pound.

So I invested in an extra three cows, sold the separator and the churn and started going to the creamery. I took milk to the Creamery for ten years. It was a dreadful nuisance, and I couldn't have managed without my mother who took over on horse-fair days, but I missed it when I gave it up. The Creamery was a unique kind of social club.

I drove a car with a primitive sort of trailer made out of the body of the gig we drove during the war. But most farmers in the fifties were still using horse or donkey-drawn carts. We queued up, sometimes for as much as an hour, and people walked around exchanging gossip. Some people arrived with a newspaper, and these were passed around so that everyone could sample them all.

Ireland isn't quite as insular – parochial even – as she was then. I remember the following exchange:

'It says on the paper there was twenty killed in a rail crash.'

'Holy God, that's terrible. Was it in Ireland?'

'No, somewhere in the world.'

Papers read, we waited, patiently or not, according to our natures. Once, a fight broke out between a lorry driver and a farmer who had tried to jump the queue. It was a hot day and each was armed with a pound of butter. These were wrapped, to start with, in greaseproof paper. Later, both combatants looked as if they'd been in a custard-pie-throwing session. The winner knelt on the other, rubbing butter on his face and into his hair. Later they went to wash it off, the best of friends again.

When there was nothing like this to enliven the wait, long discussions took place. Purity was a favourite subject – of the milk, I should add. Hygiene wasn't remarkable in the early days. I have seen a child tumble into the milk tank and be fished out again. I have seen a man drop his jacket into the milk, get it out and wring the surplus back into the tank. He was told off for this, but the milk was used.

Then progress hit the creamery. Purity tests began, in the sneaky form of spot checks. Suppliers asked one another anxiously, 'Have you passed your purity test?' Often the reply was a sad shake of the head.

But the Creamery officials struggled on, knowing that hygiene at home must be improved too. What of the cat which, pursuing a mouse across a dresser, fell into a pan of cream on a lower shelf? The old lady who owned him lifted him out by the scruff of the neck and squeezed him out like a dishcloth back into the pan. That didn't happen in Ireland, but in Yorkshire by the way. I include it for the benefit of all those who are saying to themselves, 'That could only have happened in Ireland.'

Nearer home, there was the time when I forgot to cover the cream in the dairy at night. In the morning the cream looked as if there was a pair of grey woollen gloves floating in it. It turned out to be four-teen drowned mice. I was about to tip the lot down the drain when a neighbour called. 'Waste is a sin,' she said. 'You should strain it and churn it. Who's to know?'

I hastily threw it away, mice and all, as I suspected she would have accepted it for herself. The woman was horrified. 'I never said you should use it,' she said. 'Sell it. What the eye doesn't see …'

*

As time went on, my mother became less keen on going to the Creamery for me, so I had to rely on outside help which wasn't always forthcoming. Neither Edmund nor Paddy could drive a car. I even took the milk to the Creamery on my wedding day, on my way to the hairdresser's. On that occasion though, I was allowed to jump the queue.

Not long before, I'd gone to the Creamery after a late night at a dance, and queued for an hour. Milk was scarce and I had the cans in the boot – or thought I had. When I reached the stand, I discovered the boot was empty, the milk at home. I had to drive back five miles for it, return and queue all over again. I didn't live it down for some time. One feeble joke could be made to last and last at the creamery. When some bright lad found a rubber stamp, and stamped the words EXPORT REJECT on the manager's white trousered bottom without being noticed, the story went round with embellishments for weeks.

*

At this time, the Creamery was next door to a field, now part of the cattle mart. A cow lived in this field, and her owner milked her and brought the milk in a churn on the handlebars of his bike. I have also seen him milk her, when she was going dry, in the street. He would take perhaps a quart of milk to the Creamery in a bucket.

One day when a number of people were sheltering in my car from the rain, this man passed by, driving two bullocks. 'Look at the grand cows, Dada,' piped up a little boy, face pressed to the window.

'They're not cows, they're bullocks,' said Dada. 'Cows is the lads has tits.'

There used to be a busy shop in the town, with a large orchard at the back, but no way into the street except through the shop. The owner thought it a pity to waste the grass, so he bought a heifer calf and carried her through the shop one day, wrapped in a sack, to the orchard. There she lived for many years, growing, not unnaturally, into a cow. Every year, the AI man made his way unobtrusively through the shop; every year, the cow had a calf which was carried out wrapped in a sack, and sold.

Every morning, at around 9 a.m., a man might have been seen coming out of the shop, which was a draper's by the way, with a bucket of milk which he carried down to the Creamery. In spring-time, two buckets. At last, the man who milked the cow left, and her owner decided to sell her. He thought it would attract least comment if he drove her out through the shop at night, which he did.

A party of merrymakers leaving the hotel late, told their friends next day that they'd seen a cow emerging from a draper's shop at 3 a.m. The advice they got was to take more water with it.

There was a comradeship about the Creamery, of a kind which is less common than it used to be. It was also a link between town and country. A bulk tank is a handy thing, but I'm not the only one who misses the Creamery.

*

Over the ten years when I was going to the Creamery, a great many farmers acquired cars, but a minority preferred a horse for the pur-pose. The favoured transport was a flat cart, or 'dray car', drawn by a creamery cob.

A creamery cob is, or was, a strong clean-legged animal, anywhere between 14.2 and 15.2 hands high. Ideally, it was sired by an Irish draught out of a thoroughbred pony cross. This cross could also produce a top-class riding horse, but the true creamery cob wasn't really a riding animal. It had too much action and not enough life about it. Most farmers favoured a mare, with the idea of, as the saying went, 'knocking a foal out of her' in her spare time.

Unfortunately, the foaling and calving seasons coincide, and many a mare came to the Creamery almost too wide to fit between the shafts. One of them actually foaled back into the cart she was pulling, a dedicated working mother if ever there was one. I should mention that she was weeks before her time, mares being notoriously bad at reckoning dates.

I once had a day's hunting on a mare known simply as Fogarty's Cob. She could jump like a grasshopper, and almost as suddenly. Standing facing a wooden gate, she abruptly took one step back and jumped over it, dropping her head at once to graze. I turned a backward somersault worthy of a circus act, landing, amazingly, on my feet.

Years later I bought a brown horse I called Fairfax, which made a showjumper for the great Yorkshire dealer Bert Cleminson. Bert wanted to know more of the horse's breeding and I discovered he was out of Fogarty's Cob.

Dealers looking for riding-school horses for the English trade found a rich supply at the creameries of West Clare. Villages like Doonbeg, Moyasta, Cooraclare and many more were full of hardy little animals suitable for beginners to ride. Their great advantage was that they were yoked at two years old, but not asked to do heavy work. They had learned to be biddable before they reached their full strength, were up to weight, and most were well fed and well treated.

Dealers buying horses which would never be between shafts again asked not 'Has be been ridden?' but, 'Do you take him to the creamery?' Hundreds of these cobs were bought over the years by the Doyle brothers from Limerick. They went to various riding establishments in England. I seldom bought an animal of this type, but was often asked to try one out for a buyer, to see how it behaved under a saddle. The best place for this was the old Limerick Haymarket, where there were concrete steps about eighteen inches high. Most of the cobs would literally trot up and down them, as sure-footed as goats.

The sudden leap in the cost of transport stopped this trade in its tracks. No more could horses travel in stalls on the boats; it was roll on, roll off for everything. The cost of container space ate up the profits, as it is a sad fact that a cheap horse takes up as much space as a dear one. Obviously, the cheap ones couldn't pay.

These cobs had a useful place and are sadly missed. Their hardiness, their versatility and, above all, their temperament are hard to find today. It would be interesting to know just how many international showjumpers have been bred off members of that endangered species, the creamery cob.

CHAPTER FOURTEEN

Muck and Money

I had been increasing my stock numbers – and my profits – for about five years before I began to find favour with my bank manager, and even to be offered loans I didn't need. I didn't, however, get my title deeds returned until I married.

The bank's mistrust of women farmers was echoed in Macra na Feirme, an organization for young farmers. This body ran an agricultural show, where I exhibited young horses once or twice. The standard was low, and they won prizes. These shows were known for running competitions of skill for farmers. One of these was guessing the weight of a heifer for twopence. I proffered two pennies.

'This is just for men and boys,' said the very young man in charge.

'Why?' (I'd been buying cattle for years, and felt better qualified than some of the schoolboys taking part.)

'Because that's the way it is. You can guess the weight of the cake. Or next year, you could go in for baking the best sponge.'

The idea that any man, no matter how thick, automatically knew more about farming than any woman, had some kind of Divine Right about it. It was many years before this state of things altered, and even now a woman farmer finds it difficult to be taken seriously unless she is known to have a male partner. He may be a drunken layabout; he may have no interest in farming. No matter, he is a man.

The bank manager wasn't alone in thinking that marriage was the only lifesaver for a woman with a farm. My neighbours too had a keen interest in my future (or the future of my land) and constantly suggested suitable partners. They succeeded only in making me suspect the motives of every suitor who came my way.

Two neighbours came rushing up to me at a cattle fair one day, both talking at once. They had found just the husband for me, a Protestant and, they were almost sure, an orphan. 'You wouldn't want some bitter old grave-dodger living with you,' they said.

I asked anxiously if they had told this paragon of their plans. They hadn't, but thought he would welcome the idea. 'He's not too old,' said one, 'And he has his own teeth.' Even this wasn't enough for me. They went away, disappointed.

*

When I did marry, years later, it was generally supposed that I needed extra (unpaid) help on the farm and, with luck, a couple of strong sons. This enraged both of us.

I was looking forward to having somebody to share the workload, but realized that my qualifications as a housewife were nil. I had to learn to cook, almost from scratch. I was fortunate indeed to have six stepdaughters to teach me.

When I was growing up, we always had a cook. Not necessarily a good cook, some of them were appalling, but a person capable of putting some kind of meal on the table at stated intervals. By degrees, cooks disappeared, and outside help took their place. I was sixteen when the last one departed. There followed an interval of hunger and indigestion. My mother could make only cakes, which she did excellently; my repertoire consisted of porridge and scrambled eggs. My father could make soup and curry, and, on the cook's night out, he did this. For the purpose of cooking, he first put on his hat – I don't know why. As a rule, it was a sign that he was going to do something fairly dramatic.

I remember a dinner party when I was a tiny child and supposed to be in bed. There were, I knew, silver dishes with bonbons in them on the dinner table. I slipped down to help myself, but I'd chosen the wrong moment. I heard the gong and immediately afterwards the dining-room door opened. I dived under the table where I lay, along with my mother's dog for the whole of the meal.

There was a large and probably valuable mahogany sidebord in the dining-room, on which stood a huge, heavy silver tray. Both sideboard and tray are gone long since. Anyway, the tray suddenly crashed down, sending a number of smaller silver objects flying off the sideboard. Some rolled under the table, but nobody saw me. My father got up and left the room. When he returned, he was carrying a hammer and wearing his hat. He then hammered a two-inch nail into the sideboard and stood the tray up again, leaning against the nail; after which he removed his hat and went on with his meal.

Before our first cookless Christmas, my parents anxiously discussed the preparation and cooking of a turkey. 'Surely it can't be difficult,' I said.

'You do it then,' was the answer to that, so I was relieved not to be at home on Christmas Eve.

My mother had bought a bird which was supposed to be oven ready. 'Why, it's even been stuffed,' she exclaimed in delight. Alas, it was nature's own stuffing, and I returned to find my father (wearing his hat) disembowelling the turkey over the sink with the help of a toasting fork, of all things. We had soup, curry and cake for our Christmas dinner, but my father wasn't quite beaten. He hacked the bird in pieces which we ate, first baked and later curried, for days.

The next year, we decided that a goose might be easier to deal with. I went off for a very long ride while my parents prepared it, feeling that three in the kitchen would be a crowd. The goose was too long for the oven, so my father, always resourceful, cut through its breastbone with a hacksaw and bent it into a V shape. The end product looked curious but tasted fine.

In time, my mother learned how to scramble eggs and I mastered soup and curry, but the Christmas dinner remained a toss-up for years; a gamble with an element of surprise. We amassed dozens of books of recipes, but somehow there was always something burned, something forgotten.

I discovered an ancient journal of my great-great grandmother's, a lady who lived in England almost three hundred years ago, the mother of several hungry sons. With a nib hardly broader than a hair, she sets out the menu for a 'breakfast for one hundred hungry soules'. It consisted of turkeys, geese, hams, venison pasties, mutton pasties, game pie, twenty gallons of the best beef broth and two gross of jellied hard-boiled eggs. There was much more which I've forgotten, and the ale was measured in barrels.

I think this must have been a hunt breakfast and, if it was immediately followed by the hunt, those hungry hunters must have been martyrs to ulcers and indigestion. At all events, this section is followed by a list of fearful sounding remedies for 'biliousness and colicky humours'.

My ancestress interlarded her recipes with notes about how the meal had been received. 'William left his food upon his plate, but I think he may be in love.' It's a pity that the original has been lost, but my mother copied down much of it.

'Mince pyes are sure to please. I used 2 pounds of neat's tongues parboyled and pealed, 4 pounds of good beef suett, the same of raisons, pruens and currans, 4 large Pippens, spice, verjuice and sack. I used orange, limmon and citron peal candid. The pyes did vastly please the men, who fell asleep thereafter and snored mightily.'

Some of the recipes required two or three gallons of cream, a couple of dozen eggs and a firkin of butter. Did cholesterol not affect hearts in the eighteenth century? The lady lived on until her hundredth year, and all her household survived into old age.

One of the recipes is for 'umbel pie', the dish which gave rise to the saying 'to eat humble pie'. Umbels were the heart, liver and entrails of a deer, and traditionally the huntsman's perks. While the aristocracy dined on venison, the huntsman and his family ate umbel pie. Great-great grandmama's umbel pie, surprisingly, seems to have been a sweet dish, using much the same ingredients as the mince pies, plus 'thrice the weight of the umbels in sugar'. Ugh.

She ran into difficulties in Lent, when her clergyman husband decreed that the whole household should 'abjure the fleshe of beastes for forty days, while pondering on the temporary nature of human life'. Undaunted, his wife fed him on 'mince pyes without fleshe'.

'For these,' she tells us, 'I boyled ten egges very hard and minced them with a pound of suett and a pound of currans. I then added nutmeggs, cinnamon and rosewater. The pyes sufficed the three men adequately, as I followed them with a bag pudding. In future, I will allow six eggs for eache.'

*

As I went to more and more fairs, in search of both cattle and horses, I found less time to spend at home. The horses were in fact paying for the losses made by the farm over a period of years, as well as keeping my mother and myself in comfort if not in luxury. Gradually, the farm too began to make a profit and I applied for a grant to reclaim and drain seventy acres. Around that time, I fell down stairs and seriously damaged my back.

The months that followed were both worrying and painful. I went around in a plaster cast for four months, spent six weeks in hospital, and began to wonder if I was in the wrong profession. I was obliged to spend several hours a day lying flat on my bed, chafing at the thought of all the things I should have been doing. I took up Aran knitting professionally, and used the time to knit endless sweaters, the cable needle held between my teeth, but this didn't soothe my nerves. It was time to make a decision.

I could delegate farm work as, by then, both men were capable tractor drivers. I couldn't delegate my horse-dealing. I bought a horse or two from people I trusted, sight unseen, and there wasn't anything wrong with them; but they were bought too dear, there was no room for commission for my agents and profit for me. I left my knitting and went back to the horse fairs, cross-eyed with painkillers.

There came a day when I didn't think that I could carry on, and didn't even want to. That was when I advertised the farm for sale. It was 1961, and the asking price for my 204 acres was £12,000. However, nobody was tempted, and £10,000 was my best offer. I might even have taken it, but for a salutary lesson I learned at the time.

One of my buyers owned a pub. He was most anxious to buy a farm and had been saving up for years. It was he who had offered £10,000. One evening, this man, whom I will call Chris, turned up at my house with a suitcase and asked to see me privately. I took him into the dining-room and he put his case down on the table and started trying to persuade me to accept his price for the land.

I listened fairly patiently, but said at last, 'No, I've told you I won't take ten thousand – or eleven. Twelve is the price.'

'I'll make you take ten,' said Chris. 'You won't be able to say no.' With that, he opened the suitcase with a flourish and stood back. A powerful smell of stale stout and cheap pipe tobacco filled the room. The case was stuffed with £5 notes. And yes, there was £10,000 there. Chris invited me to count it, but I declined. I thought about the fields, the garden, the house where I'd always lived, and I looked at the mound of grubby fivers which Chris was eagerly showing me. I said, 'I've changed my mind about selling. I'll take the place off the market tomorrow.'

Chris was put out. He argued. He offered another £200. I stood firm. As I was going to bed that night, I noticed that, almost without my noticing, my back had become less painful.

The lesson is too obvious to need underlining, but it has stood me in good stead. I no longer thought of market price, but of real values. This was especially true when I started keeping sheep soon after-wards. A field of standing wheat has already cost money. It will take a lot more money to convert it into loaves of bread. A failed crop can be a disaster, leaving the farmer with unpayable debts.

If you own a few sheep and prices collapse, as they did soon after the introduction of headage grants, you have options. You can sell your cull ewes for what they'll fetch, having collected all available subsidies; you can keep your ewe lambs for breeding instead. If you can't sell your wether lambs, you can eat them – or somebody else can. They can be killed and frozen and, even if they are silly cheap, you can replace them with breeding females equally cheaply. Having bought good-quality ewes, you sit tight and await better things. A lamb sold for £70 in a flying trade is no better to eat than a similar lamb worth £30 when trade is flat. The fact that an animal was expensive won't make it provide any extra dinners. A fat sheep or a fat bullock is a solid reality, easily converted into food. That's more than can be said for the mucky tokens we call money.

*

It's amazing that I've managed to write so much about my life with only a passing reference to sheep. They have been part of the scenery for so long that I find it hard now to imagine farming without them. Yet I didn't have any until a year after I had made the fateful decision to stay put.

I had been milking cows for almost as long as I could remember. The herd now numbered fifteen. My first creamery cheque was for just over £9, but now averaged around £50 a month. Not riches, but enough, just, to get by. The cows did badly, and it was a long time before I discovered why: although I liked buying and selling cattle, I hated cows. I thought them noisy, messy, smelly, stupid creatures, and I liked them even less in busy times like harvest, when I often had to milk them all by hand, as we didn't have a machine.

Sometimes I milked them on Sundays, but Paddy normally did this. He was a ploughman, not a cowman, and did it out of kindness, often after a hurling match. On these occasions, he would lead his bike by the handlebar rather than risk riding it, and wear his cap over one ear. He would sing as he milked, the same sad songs that put energy into the plough-horses. One evening after a particularly good match, I went out to help Paddy milk – I'd seen him reeling across the yard, swinging the buckets and singing tunelessly.

'Did we win, Paddy?' I asked him.

'No, we lost,' Paddy replied carefully. 'That's why I'm worse than I am,' he added.

'I'll milk one of those cows.' I reached for a bucket.

'I have them all milked.'

'Not this one. Look, she's full of milk.' The cow had lately calved and her udder looked likely to burst.

Paddy's eyes focused slowly. 'Oh God,' he said. 'I must have milked one of the others twice.'

Paddy and I agreed about cows, but Paddy didn't much like calves either. There was a kind of gloomy 'I told you so' satisfaction about him if one of them died. When Edmund was ill and Paddy was in charge of the cows and calves, he refused to help with anything that was sick. I remember him saying of a sick heifer, 'If she gets well, the best she can do is grow into a cow.' She didn't get well; she died. We had in those days to hand in all ear tags off dead animals, and I asked Paddy to secure the tag before the huntsman arrived to collect the carcass. Later, I was having breakfast when Paddy came in and, remarking 'Here's the tag,' dropped something black, hairy and cold beside my plate. The tag being firmly attached, he had cut off the ear instead.

I bought my first sheep in the face of opposition from both men and good advice from my neighbours. It was impossible to breed sheep at Crannagh, they said. The lambs would die. I insisted on having my own way and bought ten ewes. Needless to say, I knew nothing whatever about them. I had no sheds, no dog, no proper fences, no experience, no knowledge and no sense. In addition, I couldn't find any books on the subject and the farming papers were interested only in cows.

I was bewildered by the old wives' tales which abounded at the time. I thought my neighbour was joking when he warned me against cutting the lambs' tails. The good would run out of them by way of the stumps and they'd never thrive, he said. This was a warning which I disregarded from the first.

My ten ewes lambed in a twenty-acre field with huge thorny hedges and I inspected them at midnight and 5 a.m. with a flash-lamp. Needless to say, I had no enclosure where I could catch a sick ewe, and wouldn't have known what to do for her anyway.

Edmund had a fund of tales and cures which were of little practical use. When the first ewe lambed, he made collars of red tape for the lambs. 'Why?' I asked.

'The first lambs. It's always been done. It's lucky.'

'Yes, but why?'

'Because that's the way it is.'

I suspect the practice goes back to pagan times. Perhaps it averts the evil eye or propitiates the gods. Another practice I wouldn't countenance was that of draping the afterbirth over a hawthorn tree. (The afterbirth used to be called the 'haw'.) This unpleasant idea must surely have had to do with the maytree as an emblem of fertility. Anyway, I put my foot down and had the afterbirths buried. Nobody was surprised when almost half of the lambs died. The vet diagnosed lamb dysentery, I gave injections and from that day most survived, but Edmund wasn't convinced.

The weather turned cold in the second half of March and I considered bringing the ewes and lambs into the farmyard. But how to feed them? It was patiently explained to me that sheep wouldn't eat hay, and Providence had never intended them to eat meal. Grass or turnips – nothing else. I hadn't any turnips left, so I tried them with oats and they loved it. I was surprised to hear that sheep didn't drink any water and, for a day or two, I didn't offer them any. Then I began to wonder what they used for making milk and decided that a bucketful couldn't do any harm. Poor things, they mobbed me for it, and I put a trough in their shed. 'They'll die,' said Paddy. On the contrary, they did better than before.

In due course, my sheep were shorn, and I found out why two of them hadn't lambed. They were wethers. Wool was dear that year, so dear in fact that a fleece was sometimes worth more than the sheep wearing it, and the ten fleeces made £30. Ten fleeces this year would hardly make £10, but wages were a fiver a week then and way over £100 now.

*

'I think I should have a sheepdog,' I said.

'Dogs upset sheep. They sling their lambs and get on their backs and die.'

This information of course came from someone who'd never seen a good or even moderate dog at work. Nothing, but nothing, could have been more upsetting to a sheep than Paddy and me practising a bit of midwifery. 'We landed him,' said Paddy, wiping his hands and looking proudly at the limp lamb. The ewe was firmly held down by a knee on her neck, I was trying to make the lamb suck. All this was after I'd run down the ewe, caught her and had an all-in wrestling match which I won by a narrow margin.

I took a turn at holding the ewe down while Paddy stood bent double and milked her into the lamb's mouth. The ewe bleated and struggled as hard as she could. The ram I'd bought (for ten sheep, two of them wethers!), hearing one of his wives in trouble, attacked Paddy from behind, hitting him fair and square. I looked up and saw Paddy riding away on the ram's back, still grimly clutching the lamb. He was carried quite a distance before he fell off. After that, I had to deal with new-born lambs unassisted.

I sold my first crop of lambs well. I was horse-dealing full time as well as keeping cattle and growing crops, so I didn't want extra breeding ewes. The handful I had then cost me more headaches than the three hundred and fifty I eventually kept. So I went to a fair and bought sixty lambs. I think my guardian angel was working overtime that day; I knew less than nothing about store lambs. They doubled their money off grass.

My next deal was less lucky. The sheep fair clashed with the horse fair at Ballinasloe, which I couldn't afford to miss, so I sent Edmund to buy lambs for me. He was anxious to buy good ones and afraid of the consequences if he didn't, so he bought from my cousin, thinking to please me. My cousin knew less, if possible, about sheep than I did, and was making his first and last foray into sheepkeeping.

The twenty lambs were Border Leicester crossed with something even larger – perhaps those outsized animals which used to be found in Roscommon and nowhere else. I turned them out on new grass and they grew – and grew. When they were about as big as donkeys, some nine months later, they still weren't fat. I took them to the mart which had just replaced the fair. They could easily have stepped out of their pen. So enormous were they that several people asked me what the new breed was called. After answering truthfully for a while, I told somebody they were called Polled Flockmasters. I got a good price and found out afterwards that word had gone round that Polled Flockmasters were the sheep of the future.

I kept clear of sheep until the following spring, when I took fifty lambs belonging to a neighbour to eat turnips for £15 a month. After a time it occurred to me that if there was room for him to make profit after paying rent, I should be making it. So I bought the sheep and my neighbour was pleased because they were, he said, getting too fat. There turned out to be a reason for this. Nearly all of them were in lamb and the lambs survived. My neighbour had to take a lot of slagging from his friends about that.

My unluckiest purchase was made when I was on a holiday in Connemara. I bought twenty fine big hogget ewes off a mountain near Oughterard, encouraged by a tempting price. I noticed they had rudimentary horns. 'I'd like them better without the horns,' I said.

'There's no extra charge for them,' said the farmer.

I took the sheep home and turned them into a small well-fenced paddock with a rick of hay in it. In the morning, they were marching about on top of the rick, which was, I suppose, the nearest they could get to a mountain. I went to get a ladder to chase them down, carelessly leaving the gate open. When I got back, they'd gone.

I knew nothing of the homing instinct of mountain sheep. They had set off for their native Connemara, always travelling by road and always in the right direction. They did this again and again, and each time I recovered them there was one less than before. When the number was down to seventeen, I sold the rest at a loss.

Keeping sheep efficiently is an all-the-year-round task. The myth persists that 'lambing time' is a nightmare, reminiscent of an emergency ward after a cosmic disaster. For the rest of the year, sheep and shepherd recover from the experience. I've often been asked how I fill my time when lambing's over and 'there's no work with the sheep'. There's always work with the sheep, but if you like them, you don't mind. I did mind, very much, working a seven-day week with cows.

*

I learned what I know about sheep from my husband, John, although I'd been keeping them for years before I was married. John wasn't a sentimental man, but like me he loved sheep and sheepdogs. He would glance at one of a hundred ewes and say, 'She's carrying dead lambs,' or 'She's getting pneumonia,' or 'She's going to die.' He was always right; the ewe that was going to die always did. I would make a fuss and insist on the vet being fetched, but a sheep which has made up its mind to die usually does. John couldn't explain how he knew these things, but by degrees I learned to recognize them myself – I don't know how. It's more a matter of sympathy than knowledge.

Sympathy and sentiment are of course different things. Sentiment is the emotion felt by two families who swap pet lambs before killing and eating them. You couldn't possibly eat dear little Rambo, could you? But your friends could, and you could eat their pets. I also knew two families who swapped rabbits they couldn't bear to kill.

I remember seeing a little boy carrying a black rabbit down the street. Another boy joined him and asked, 'Are you going to eat him?'

'I'm going to keep him, you bloody cannibal,' was the reply. Sentiment of a kind, but understandable.

I was as sentimental as the next when I started breeding sheep, there being something which appeals to one's maternal instinct about an abandoned lamb. Agnes was a typical case. I found Agnes, abandoned by her mother, in a ditch. I brought her back to life against all the odds, spending most of a night feeding her with warm milk, drop by drop. Agnes was a short-backed, tubby lamb, of mixed ancestry, and the best place for her would have been the freezer. I was well aware of this, but I stubbornly kept her for breeding. Agnes produced one short-backed, tubby lamb every year until she, providentially, died.

A farmer of my acquaintance kept a pet lamb for eleven years; when toothless, she lived mainly in the kitchen and ate porridge among other things. But, unlike Agnes, she was a fine specimen and a prolific mother.

Sympathy is nursing a sick animal – and knowing when to give up. Sentiment is keeping a poor old horse turned out in a field all the year round without company or care, because you can't bear to put him down. Not kindness but cruelty. I'm sure that when you start thinking of farm animals as 'stock units' you lose touch with reality. It may be all right if you deal in thousands; in a small enterprise it's a mistake. As I write this, my ewes are lambing; it's midnight, time for a last visit to the shed. There the lights are on and the sheep are lying down asleep. As I walk among them, hardly any bother to get up. I talk quietly to them, which may be silly but does no harm and may do good.

I have the same sympathy with horses, dogs, even bullocks, but not cows. Accordingly, all cows treat me with suspicion. If you have to deliver a calf or lamb, the task is much easier if the mother trusts you, because she will relax. Some vets inspire trust in their patients, just as some doctors do; others don't.

You have to like sheep to put up with them, as they can try your patience to the last. Highest in irritation value comes the lamb which can, but won't suck; this is followed by the ewe which could, but won't get up. Almost as bad is the lamb which jumps straight back into the bramble-filled ditch you've spent half an hour getting him out of.

It's obvious that mutual understanding and trust are important for a dog and his master. I believe they can be developed between shepherd and sheep to the advantage of both.

CHAPTER FIFTEEN

Never a Dull Moment?

In my late twenties I seemed to buy a lot of horses by torchlight or under street lamps. This was doing things the hard way, but I simply didn't have the daylight hours to spare – except in midsummer, when there were more of them.

I bought three chestnut three-year-old geldings off the land, more or less in the dark. I could see a donkey lurking nearby, but thought nothing of it. I arranged to have the horses delivered by lorry – after dark, of course. Horses are gregarious creatures and, if you need to catch some, they will follow one another in from the field. Not so donkeys. If you own two and you think that, by catching one, you can move both, think again. But horses sometimes form the most violent attachments to donkeys, being heartbroken when they are separated from them. Some people borrow a donkey to keep a young horse company. This may be a good idea, or it may not.

The three colts arrived in my yard, travelling loose in the lorry, and I switched on some lights. I shut the gate as the three clattered down the ramp, as all were unbroken and I thought I'd drive them into a large shed for the night. The donkey was with them. I said, 'I didn't buy the donkey.'

'We had to bring him because the Prince Richard colt wouldn't go in without him,' said the driver.

'Well, catch the donkey and put it back in the lorry.' As the donkey didn't want to be reloaded, it planted its feet and began to bray. At once, the Prince Richard colt flattened the stable door as if it had been cardboard, charged out and both he and the donkey bounded back into the lorry. In order to get the colt out, we had to drag the donkey out too. It was plain that this could go on all night. In the end, I had to keep the donkey until I got the horse halter-broken, and even then it was hard to separate them. When the donkey had gone, the horse pined for him.

I also had a terrible job separating a mare from a donkey when I bought her. In this case, the donkey couldn't have cared less, but the mare became quite frantic and nearly kicked herself out of the trailer on the way home. I think she had managed to persuade herself that the donkey was her foal, but the donkey was less suggestible.

*

Lorries were scarce in the fifties and not designed for carrying horses. Few were covered, not many had ramps. If there was no loading bank at one's destination, the horses had to jump down. I engaged a lorry, sight unseen, to take three young horses to a show. It turned out to have open, slatted sides, having been designed for sugar beet. The corners were tied with string, and I mean string, not the invaluable coloured baling twine which is almost unbreakable. No, this was the hairy, tarry variety.

I don't think I'd have gone, but one horse was owned by a schoolboy who would have been bitterly disappointed if I'd refused. We travelled with the horses, holding their heads so as to keep them clear of the sides. We hung onto them like grim death as the rickety, swaying contraption rattled and banged its way along. It was a horrible journey and going home was worse, as the driver had spent the day in the bar and drove with reckless abandon.

On my first trip to Buttevant, I saw what must have been the most dangerous conveyance ever for carrying a horse. It was an ordinary, flat tractor-trailer, on which four gates had been erected, tied in a square with the inevitable string. They were no more than three feet high. The two front corners were tied to the towing bar of the trailer with light rope. In this improvised pen stood a 16.2 hands unbroken brown filly, three-quarter bred. Not the sort one would want to take risks with. As if that wasn't enough, her halter rope was tied to the seat of the tractor with a black knot and there was, of course, no safety cab.

The driver of the tractor was about seventy-five, and a bit stiff on his legs. I watched in growing alarm as he tried to open the knot. At last, I offered a pocket knife. 'Take your time, child of grace,' he said, 'The Man who made time made lots of it.' He opened the knots and accepted the knife to cut the string which held the pen together. I meant to buy the filly if she didn't break a leg. He pulled the rope, and the filly, snorting a little, jumped down onto the tarmac. I did buy her and never regretted it.

My first trailer cost £50 and was dear at the price. It was a tall, flimsy, two-wheeled affair, and only the fact that I'd driven a hundred miles to see it made me buy it. (I should mention in passing that this reasoning is unsound, but influences more buyers than you would think.)

The best thing about it was that it was as light as a feather and my Morris Minor pulled it easily. I took a horse to a hunter trial in it, and had the nasty experience of having a wheel come off and bowl down the road in front of me. I don't know why they do this, but they do. For some reason, neither car nor trailer turned over, nor did the horse fall. He relaxed inside it at an acute angle until somebody arrived with a lorry jack.

I was nervous after that of taking the trailer to Kilrush fair – few motorists carry lorry jacks – so I hired a heavy double box. This meant hiring a car too, a fine big gangster-movie type thing with an instrument panel like an airliner. When I tried to haul two horses home, however, I realized the garage man had been right when he'd said the car wouldn't pull the socks off you. I had to leave one behind and go back for him. It was a great day when I was able to afford a bigger car and a double trailer.

It's worth mentioning that for many years I didn't own a car that would lock, as I'd generally managed to lose the key. The car was left with a change of clothes and sometimes a saddle in it all day. I never had anything taken out of it, and when I lost my watch in Limerick fair, it was picked up and returned to me.

During two long bank strikes, I went to the fairs, like everyone else, with my pockets stuffed with banknotes. I remember one particularly sultry day at Kilrush, being amused at the 'big' dealers, sweating in their jackets because of the enormous sums of cash they were carrying. One man, almost fainting with the heat, took off his jacket – but put on a pair of wellies. This seemed more than eccentric in a heatwave, but he paid for his next purchase with a wad of notes which he extracted from one of his boots.

I myself had £600 distributed in the pockets of my jeans, and was relieved when most of it was converted into horseflesh. I never heard of anyone being robbed at this time.

The same year at Ballinasloe, the owner of a new Land-Rover and Rice trailer left them unlocked all day, as the theft of such things was unheard of. Some chancer quite openly loaded up two horses, took them to Dublin and embarked with them for Birkenhead. The Land-Rover and trailer were left tidily and unharmed in the North Wall car park. On the driver's seat was a note with 'Thanks' scribbled on it.

Also at Ballinasloe that year, a man from the North of Ireland, having sold both his horses on the Sunday, set off for home with his car and trailer. He was alone and happy, so he turned his radio up full volume. He was somewhere between Longford and Cavan by the time the courting couple in the trailer managed to attract his attention ...

*

The beginner's luck which tided me over my first few years with horses couldn't last. It came apart with a spectacular failure. This concerned a mare called Echo.

Marigold, while not doing much for my bank account, was a mild nuisance compared with Echo. I was gaining confidence (fatal) as I got glowing reports about the earlier horses. Not one of the first half dozen had failed to win in some capacity, and one was well on her way to becoming an international showjumper. I thought I was all set to make a fortune.

The Echo Valley is an eerie spot in the Arra Mountains. Like the Roaring Glen in the same area, it is a deep river gorge. In one spot, if you shout, answers come back from several directions. Out hunting one day, I saw a big, good-looking chestnut mare trotting about in the field near the glen. When hounds went away, she went straight down the valley side after them, through the river and up the other side, with a couple of stag-like bounds. I made a note of the place, went back and bought her, so I had nobody to blame but myself.

Echo had been broken and gone in harness. She didn't put a foot wrong for a fortnight, then she suddenly hurled me off as I was riding her out of the yard. This was so unexpected – a dropped shoulder and a buck backwards – that I hadn't a chance. Bruised and angry, I remounted and rode her for hours. No trouble. My confidence rather shaken, I waited for other signs of vice but there were none. So I took her out hunting and refused profit on what I'd given for her. She went well. On the way home, she suddenly threw me off on the road. She didn't gallop away. I picked myself up, remounted with difficulty and rode home.

Echo behaved nicely for so long after that that I thought I was safe. Then she had a go at a meet. This was on the forecourt of a garage. She was standing quite still, when a quiver seemed to travel down the reins to my hands. I grabbed the front of the saddle and hung on. The people present were treated to a Wild-West display, while only the fear of being hurt again kept me desperately clinging to the saddle. Some shouted 'Hold on!' Others shouted 'Jump off!' There was a crack as the girth tabs pulled clean out of the saddle, and saddle and I crashed down on the concrete. This time, Echo turned and tried to savage me. Somebody caught her and she calmed down.

Knowing I'd never ride her again if I didn't do it that day, I led her home, got another saddle and fixed her up with side reins and a 'bucking rein'. She had bucked so hard that she'd broken two of her shoes in half. She made a half-hearted attempt to start something, and knew at once that I'd tackled her so that she couldn't get her head down. So she ran away instead.

I pulled, Echo pulled harder and away we went. She galloped about two miles down the road, out of control. I kept her to the left of the road and hoped we wouldn't meet anything. The road was a dead end, leading only to Lough Derg. As we tore downhill, gathering speed, we met an old man plodding towards us, leading a cow on a rope. The old man walked on one side of the road, the cow on the other. Both had their minds on other things. Between them, the slack rope stretched, perhaps a foot from the road. Echo raced straight over it and we missed a horrible fall by – luck?

She kept going, and we reached the long downhill slope which ends in the lake. I dragged at the reins in vain as she plunged into the water, which was soon halfway up her sides. I was wondering whether she was going to swim to Dromineer when she suddenly came to her senses and let me haul her round. She then trotted home quite pleasantly.

On the way, we overtook the old man with the cow, still plodding along.

The next morning, when at last I was able to crawl downstairs, my father forbade me ever to ride Echo again. I protested, but really I was glad of an excuse. My father's veto was backed by several friends who called to see if I was alive. When I could get about again, I started working Echo in harness. This I did to save her life as I was determined that nobody would ride her again, and even then, I was reluctant to sell her for beef. Then one day, when she was at grass, I saw her indulge in a fit of bucking until she was exhausted. She also dropped on her knees and tore up mouthfuls of earth. The vet thought she had a brain tumour, and she went to the knackers. I don't know if she did have a tumour, but I believe she was mad – actually insane.

*

From time to time afterwards, I bought horses which weren't all they were supposed to be. I learned to cut my losses. In Thurles fair, many years after Echo had dented my nerve, I bought a horse which was exactly what he was said to be and made another expensive mistake.

This fellow was an ideal police horse, and I might easily have sent him straight to England and seriously have damaged my reputation. I bought him with another, they were half brothers, both good-looking, a bay and a brown. The price was reasonable, but not low enough to make me suspicious. I asked if the bay, the older of the two, had been hunted. 'Oh yes, he's well known with the hunt.' This was true, but not quite in the accepted sense.

'Is he good over banks?' I asked.

The owner looked hurt. 'I guarantee,' he said patiently, 'that wherever your huntsman goes, that horse will go.' This was also true.

I was pleased with my purchase. He was big, handsome and had a good mouth. I rode him about at home and popped him over some fences. No problem. I began to think of keeping him for myself. I clipped him out and took him to a meet near the ill-omened Echo Valley. He was as good as gold at the meet, and, when hounds started to run, he jumped his way forwards until he was just behind the huntsman and rather too close to him. I discovered how right his last owner had been. Wherever the huntsman went, so did my horse. Attempts to stop him resulted in wild rears and backward rushes. I have never been on the back of a horse which had so completely mastered the art of rearing without falling over backwards. I clung round his neck with both arms as he backed rapidly towards the edge of the gorge on his hind legs.

Of course, this manoeuvre beat me, as it was meant to do. For the next two hours, he followed the huntsman as closely as if he'd been tied to his horse's tail. When we reached the road, I thought I'd better take him home before he killed me – or somebody else. But my efforts to go home before the huntsman did were nearly fatal, as he ran backwards on his hindlegs across the Dublin road. A certain lorry driver may well remember that day. Reunited with the huntsman, he gave no more trouble.

There was a dealer out that day who was unwise enough to offer me cost for my horse. He was sold on – to the London Police.

*

Clyde, as he was called, was about my unluckiest purchase at Thurles fair, the nearest to home and held every month. My first visit to the fair was to sell a workhorse called Barney, a tall, narrow animal which was always thin and bad in his coat. When I rode into the town, I almost wished I'd stayed at home. Horses filled half of Liberty Square and the street as far as the river. Beyond the Suir bridge, hundreds more jammed the streets and pavements, away past the Cathedral. Farther down, a solid mass of tinkers' horses were gathered at the gateway of the Protestant church. No Thurles girl in her right mind got married on a 'first Tuesday', and funerals added a whole new di-mension to the chaos.

I was stopped in the square by an old farmer who asked Barney's price, also why he was so thin. 'He's always like that,' I said. 'I want £40 for him.'

The farmer looked him over and remarked that all the strong horses were gone. 'You can't eat them and have them,' he said. I said that, although thin, Barney was very strong, and got a look of scorn, tinged with sympathy.

'When I was a lad,' said the farmer, 'I had two great bears of horses, as strong as castles. When they'd lean into the collar, God almighty, they'd shift Ireland.' Barney couldn't compete with that sort of thing, but I managed to sell him for £35.

Later that day, I bought a bay filly for £30. She looked like a bargain and was even better than she looked. This mare, Vanity, was the first I 'vetted' myself. I'd found out at Limerick that it was impos-sible to get a horse examined in a fair, so I'd watched vets at work, asked questions and now tried doing it myself.

My first half-dozen horses weren't vetted at all. By chance, they were all sound. So was Vanity. I went over her legs, peered into her eyes, studied her teeth, backed and twisted her about and hoped to goodness I hadn't forgotten anything. 'Do you know where I could take this filly to lunge her?' I asked the farmer who had bought Barney.

'You could try the shoe-shop,' he said. I was learning not to be surprised by anything, merely asking the way to the shoe-shop. It was Maher's, at the end of the square, and I rather shyly asked the manager if he could help. It was Mr Maher himself and I'd gone to the right place. He bred the Grand National winner Quare Times and had land on the edge of the town. He told me I could gallop horses in his fields at any time, and I did so for years.

Mr Maher was a quiet-spoken man with a dry humour and plenty of stories to tell. One was about a young horse-dealing vet who lodged over a cobbler's shop in the town. He had only just set up in practice and wasn't allowed to advertise, so he put a notice in the cobbler's window: HORSES SOLD AND HEALED.

When I'd examined Vanity and paid for her, I bought a carthorse to replace Barney. Then I went in search of my lorry driver. It took me two hours to find him and he was legless. Later, I heard him telling somebody that he'd bought the two horses for me. Legless or not, he drove home. My father happened to be out walking when he heard the lorry careering down the drive, crashing into potholes while the horses were flung about in the back. He had quite a lot to say to the driver, and I've seldom seen anyone sober up so quickly.

The day I bought Vanity, I asked the price of a nice brown horse which was too dear for me. I hung about, reluctant to leave him, and asked the owner how he was bred.

'He's by Single Corpse.'

'He can't be. There can't be a stallion called Single Corpse.'

'There is so then and he's a hell of a good horse. Anybody'll tell you.'

Back home, I looked him up in the stallion register. Signal Corps.

There were some good stallions around Thurles. Captain Barton owned three of them and he used to tow them to the fair behind a trap drawn by another. There they 'stood' in the Hotel yard for the day, covering mares of all kinds.

A good sire around that area was King Justice, sire of my best-known police horse, Sandown. Sandown, many times winner of the award for Police Horse of the Year, was a natural for the job. He cost me £135, but that was many years after I had to leave the Single Corpse horse behind. I bought Sandown with his brother, Royal Justice, and his sister, Erica, all from one man. He lived on the edge of the turf bogs and, while the two geldings were housed and fit, the mare was out and looked wretched. Her owner assured me she'd soon mend. When I asked what she'd been living on, he said, 'Fresh air, spring water and rushes.' Seeing my expression, he added, 'They were the best of rushes.'

CHAPTER SIXTEEN

From Point to Point

Saddlery was hardly the word for the assortment of tack worn by the horses at the fairs. Strange bits were unearthed and polished up: long-cheeked Hannoverian pelhams, military reversibles and rubber snaffles with no rubber left on them. I have even been asked to ride a colt with a round 'Chifney' leading bit in his mouth. I refused. I have encountered strange saddles too: great army saddles with wooden panels and blankets underneath, more suited to pack animals, half-pound saddles whose stirrups I could scarcely get a toe into, even a battered Western saddle, only lacking a lariat.

I always rode on a flat type of saddle without knee-rolls at home. You could lie across one of these on a young horse while he decided whether to accept you weight or not. Lying across a modern saddle would be, at best, painful, and I felt trapped on a hollow seat, unable to bale out fast in an emergency. I wouldn't, however, go so far as a farmer who was showing his horse barebacked in Kilrush, although it wore an obviously redundant martingale, tied in a knot.

'I never use a saddle,' he said. 'They're treacherous old things – they could trap you and kill you in a minute.'

At the other extreme was an anxious young man in Thurles fair, whose fear was evidently communicating itself to his horse, which curvetted about, chewing its bit and snorting. I noticed with alarm that the young man had tied his feet into his stirrup irons with his shoelaces. I might never have bought that horse, but I was so anxious that the young man should be untied before it threw him, that I asked for a ride. He agreed eagerly and the horse, named Blarney Stone, was a successful showjumper after I sold him.

This reminds me of a gallant hunting farmer who thought he'd ride his hunter in the half-bred race at our point-to-point. He was a poor horseman who used to slide off over his horse's tail quite often when it jumped onto banks. Provided with a lightweight saddle and surcingle by the jockey's valet, he saddled up his horse. He then got a leg up and asked a friend to fasten the surcingle round his legs as well as round the saddle – tie him on, in fact. The surcingle wasn't long enough, and the stewards were alerted while his friend went in search of some rope. He fell off at the first fence and walked back, complaining that, but for the stewards' interference, he would have won.

The first point-to-point I remember was in – I think – 1935. I was holding my nurse's hand and running with her in order, she said, to see someone killed. There was a race in progress, and the runners were approaching a notorious double bank with a deep drain on either side. We arrived panting, and joined the crowd waiting hungrily for thrills and spills. I can recall waving legs as horses rolled on the ground, but nobody was killed that day.

Point-to-pointing in Ireland in the thirties was like the cross-country section of a three-day-event done on half-fit horses and with no safety regulations or rules. Much of the course was out of sight of the crowd, and once round was the rule. 'Out in the country', weights could be handed to a friend to be collected on the way back; flags could be missed and corners cut.

I have seen a man thrown off his horse by the rider beside him who simply caught him by the foot and lifted it over the saddle. Nobody was hurt and the culprit was disqualified, but his action enabled a horse to win which he had backed to beat his own.

In different places at different times, I've seen a starter so drunk he couldn't sit on his hack, and another who was carried halfway round the course with the runners. I have seen two grounded riders settling an argument with their fists in the middle of a ploughed field. It was all part of the fun.

The old course at Carrick, where the hill was a natural grandstand, crossed the public road. My mother vividly remembered seeing a race there, won by the nurse from the workhouse riding the priest's horse. The 'new' course at Grange, alongside the Galway road for much of its length, was ploughland for a mile of its three-and-a-bit. The fences included trappy single banks, a stone wall and an appalling water-jump lined with sleepers and with the flimsiest of take-off fences. It divided two ploughed fields where we raced on the muddy headlands. One lady used to sit in her car with a rug over her head when her son was riding, only coming out when the cheering told her the race was over.

When I was about fifteen, I was offered a ride in the maiden race on a three-year-old filly. A flat-sided brown, she looked as if a sharp five furlongs at Phoenix Park would suit her nicely. I had a gallop on her, and discovered that she jumped toes first, without bending her knees. Not at all the thing for a three-and-a-half-mile bank course. To my great disappointment, I wasn't allowed to accept the ride, and the young man who did was carried in on a stretcher.

I was nineteen when I first rode in a point-to-point. The event, inaccurately named the 'Sportsman's Race', was for half-breds and took place at the end of the programme. There were nine competitors of which four finished. One of these was my friend Joan. I was relieved to see her passing the post as I'd grave doubts about her horse, a borrowed brown animal called Shenanigan. Never was a horse less well named. He was a lethargic creature, mainly Irish draught; he'd a big jump in him, but a big stick was required to get it out, and shenanigans weren't his thing. The start was delayed while a rider topped up with Dutch courage in the bar. He fell off at the first fence.

There was a ladies' allowance of 7lbs, bringing the weights down to twelve stone. I weighed nine stone, Joan about seven. In spite of ordinary saddles and clothes, our leadcloths were so heavy we could hardly lift them. There was a wild stampede for the first fence, then the ploughed ground began to sort the field out. The first big bank brought down three and the water two more. The rest of us hung on.

It seemed a very long way. It was pouring with rain and growing dusk when we finished; it had been raining on and off for weeks. I got a faceful of mud from the leader at the last fence and wasn't sure where the winning-post was. My mare Matilda and I were a decent third.

My neighbours were charitable and gave us a great welcome. Mind you, I don't know why anyone was insane enough to back any of us. The whipper-in on his grey horse cleared the course at the finish of each race, galloping up the straight, scattering stray children and dogs. As he led us, soaking wet and plastered with mud from head to foot, back to the paddock, I heard a woman say, 'Imagine. The grey horse has all the races won.'

The following year, the race was a calmer affair, although run in the dusk. I managed to finish second, but never won a race. The riders wore 'hunting attire', which could mean anything. One or two sported colours. The jockey's valet had only one cap to offer and two riders almost came to blows over it. The winner of the argument wore the crash skull, the loser put on the silk cover like a sunbonnet, with the strings tied under his chin. Neither was concerned with the finish. The horse of the bonneted one galloped off the course and plunged into the Nenagh River.

*

Horse are great swimmers, as any cowboy movie will show you. As a small child, I was taken to Whitegate in County Clare to see some cattle and horses being swum across Lough Derg to Island More. The families who lived there, surviving on what they could grow and on eel fishing, had a heavy rowing-boat. They tied a cow to the stern to lead the other cattle and the horse. The cow was red and white, with great spreading horns, and swam unconcernedly behind the boat. The horse followed, with the bullocks, fairly willingly.

I got a ducking myself at one of those hair-raising point-to-points. My horse, the showjumper Sugar Bush, was 15 hands high and three years old. She could gallop and stay, but was a shocking ride over banks. If she could see over, she flew them, landing in the ditch on the far side if there was one. If she couldn't see over, she kicked back at them. This is all right in theory, but she generally missed. An accurate kick back lifts a horse yards, a missed one drops him as if he'd fallen out of a tree.

Sugar Bush had had a fortnight's concentrated schooling. She jumped perfectly until we reached that deadly water jump, where another horse cannoned into her in mid-air, sending her crashing through the wing and into the river of which the stream was a tributary. I landed first, at the bottom of four feet of muddy water. Sugar Bush sat on me briefly, then fortunately decided to move away. Yes, I know I said horses were good swimmers; this one was more of a sinker.

As I squelched back to the paddock, people asked me, 'Did you fall off?' 'Where's your horse?' and even, 'Did you get a wetting?'

*

I was under the impression that our point-to-point was typical of the sport, and was disillusioned when I went to visit a cousin who was the long-time master of a south of England pack.

It was May, and I was asked to act as fence steward at a local point-to-point. The course, which would look old-fashioned today, was 'once round' with natural cut-and-laid fences. I was amazed at the neatness of everything. It seemed more like a proper steeplechase meeting. Another surprise was the segregation of the sexes. Ladies' races were new to me.

I'd heard of them, of course. I could remember my mother's horror when she realized that her precious teenage daughter was going to compete against a lot of rough men. Men who might even be heard to utter a naughty word occasionally. Lady riders, she believed, confined themselves to exclaiming 'Drat!' 'Bother!' or, in extreme cases, 'Damn!'

I had already been buying and selling horses in fairs for two years at the time, and cattle for longer than that. Besides being immune to oaths, I knew that the age of chivalry was by no means dead and also that there was no chivalry at all among women. Now, about ten years later, I saw them collecting, wearing fur coats over their colours, smoking, talking, very much at ease. 'Darling,' they cried, 'How are you? Are you terribly well?'

The answer to this was, 'Oh, my dear, revoltingly so.'

I was asked to stand on a road which the runners had to cross, and make sure that nobody missed a flag. A soft job, I thought, as I drove back to my post in a Land-Rover for the fourth time. The next race was the ladies' event and I could hear high-pitched abuse two fields away. Two young women, sworn rivals and deadly enemies, were approaching at the head of the field.

On the road, which they reached together, the smaller lady's horse ran out and cannoned into the other. Both had to swerve and pull up, while three more runners went on into the lead. Neither said bother, or even damn. Instead, they hurled threats and abuse as they wrenched their horses round that would have made a bargee blush. They forced their mounts over the hedge from a standstill and galloped away, still screaming at each other. Another rider actually pulled up in order to yell at me, 'Report those bitches or I'll report *you*.' I didn't.

Racing in the Home Counties was disappointing in some ways. The horses were so often worn-out chasers, nothing with any improvement in it. It seemed to me like a bad imitation of steeplechasing, rather than the nursery for chasers that my own country was.

*

For many years I had an annual holiday in England, spending time with people who had bought horses from me. Generally I went in the short gap between hay and harvest – my May trip was for a wedding. Spring was a busy time.

The point-to-point should have been a warning to lie low, but it wasn't. (I had been reported for failing to report the warring women, as warned.) But no, I was landed with the job of judging in a small show a week later.

Dealers should never be tempted to judge at shows. I was to be asked to do so many times in Ireland, but always refused firmly. The snags range from discouraging canvassers to accidentally giving an award to an animal you have owned briefly and failed to recognize. I have hardly ever heard anyone say a good word for a judge unless, of course, he had been given first prize. Then it is different. The judge is a sound man, discerning and right-minded. Anyone mad enough to judge in his own area could be subjected to abuse and even threats; I have seen and heard it happen.

In England, I thought I would be safe. The show was a local affair, the prizes small, the publicity almost nil.

I was not, let it be said, the first choice. The lady intended for the job chickened out at the last moment. She said she had tonsillitis. Perhaps she had. I reckon she lost her nerve.

The friends I was staying with didn't consult me. I was no more than twenty and had been dealing in a small way for three years. I heard my host talking on the telephone, but couldn't have guessed that I was the subject.

'... Of course she will – she'd love to judge ... Certainly she's capable; she's a bloodstock breeder from Ireland ...'

Ireland? I listened more closely. But I didn't breed bloodstock.

'Yes, she's an expert on ponies.' (I hated ponies.) 'I'll ask her, but the answer's definitely yes, she will judge.'

'Who will?' I asked.

'You will.'

Protests were in vain. 'Just a few little ponies – nothing to it,' said my host airily.

The only little thing was the ring, which was more suited to a dog show. I stood quaking in the middle of it, with a scornful ring steward, old enough to be my grandfather, holding a basket of rosettes. All the rest of the space was occupied by a milling throng of ponies. Under 13.2 was the height limit; the smallest could have walked under a dinner table. Some were ridden by weeping tots, others by hard-bitten little girls of twelve or more. I stared at them, horrified. 'Where do I start?' I muttered to the steward. He shrugged his shoulders.

'Walk on,' I said, as firmly as I could. Some did. One pony grazed its way along, another firmly backed out of the ring. I began to gain a little confidence. There were twenty-three ponies left, and I sorted out about a dozen obvious no-hopers and asked them to leave the ring. That was my first serious mistake.

I got the remainder to walk and trot round in the confined space. Then I removed two that were lame and one which was thinking about kicking the pony behind. Mistake number two.

Judging the remainder was easier. I stood three in front and five behind – there were eight rosettes. The difficulty was to place first and second. They were both greys, very much alike.

Nervous of spending too much time, I examined the teeth of each. One was five years old, the other had long, yellow fangs, deeply pitted and grooved. I gave first prize to the five-year-old. My dealing experience had taught me to place little value on an old horse, however brilliant. I had made my third and most serious mistake.

Outside the ring, I was mobbed by the mothers of the tiny children I had sent out at the beginning. Most of them would have been more at home on rocking-horses. I tried to reason with them – the mothers, not the tots – noticed the steely glint in their eyes, and fled.

Next came the mothers of the no-hopers. How, I was asked, did I expect a child to have a successful showing career if discouraged right from the start? And who was I anyway? And what did they know about ponies in Ireland? And what was this rubbish about bloodstock? And how old was I?

I had never been taught that useful maxim of the Duke of Wellington's: never apologize – never explain. Muttering apologies and explanations, I made it as far as the secretary's tent. There I collapsed into a deck chair which, as in a bad movie, also collapsed with me folded up inside it. From this position of weakness I had to ward off the final attack, from the mother of the rider of the old pony.

Didn't I know who she was? Didn't I know the five-year-old had never won anything. Didn't I know what the old pony had won? Didn't I realize it had been supreme champion at the Royal Blankshire?

Here the secretary made matters worse: 'I doubt if Marjorie would remember as far back as that. It was pre-war.' The lady's wrath being diverted, I struggled out of the deck-chair and escaped.

Yes, judges should be elderly, able and thick-skinned. Since then I have successfully avoided judging any animals except the childrens' pets at a dog show. Even there, the atmosphere was charged with menace.

An old friend of mine, a marvellous judge, was asked to officiate at a lightweight hunter class when he was well over seventy. He rode all but one of the dozen animals presented; a Dales pony, hairy-legged and about fifteen hands high. 'Why didn't you judge my horse?' demanded the lady owner afterwards.

'He's in the wrong class. He's a Native Pony, not a hunter.'

'Nonsense. I've hunted him twice a week all season.'

To which the exasperated judge replied, 'Well, what do you expect me to do about that? Burst into tears?' Horse and rider flounced out of the ring. Judging is a job for heroes.

CHAPTER SEVENTEEN

Horses Change My Life

I was in my thirties by the time making a living ceased to be a non-stop punishing struggle. So it was for all farmers in Ireland in the fifties and sixties – I certainly wasn't alone. My horses saved me from disaster again and again, although the bank manager found this impossible to believe, even when confronted with figures. Farming was so bad that any spare money was usually spent on the only paying proposition – the cows. I would have been allowed to borrow to buy more cows, not to fill my horse contracts. Everywhere I went buying, the cows were fat, the horses thin. I bought a miserably thin brown colt which was drawing milk to the creamery; a narrow, high-withered creature which looked less than his height.

The Milkman, as I named him, was too sharp for the two elderly brothers who owned him. One would lead him nervously by the bridle while the other clung to the milk cans, saying, 'Whoa blood. Whoa the wild one,' in soothing tones. They were pleased to sell the thin youngster and bought an elderly, heavy mare. This one went stone blind, but continued to draw the milk-cart, regardless.

I collected The Milkman from the farm, complimenting the brothers pointedly on a lovely green field on which he had certainly not been grazing. 'Ah, that field would fatten a bicycle,' said one brother. 'No, that wouldn't be possible,' said the other, more down to earth.

Generally, my countrymen aren't lacking in imagination. I have been warned to mind the telegraph wires when I was jumping a horse I meant to buy. This suggested a leap of ten feet or so. Occasionally, I have met someone with a truly literal mind. I bought an emaciated colt which I called Castaway, and discovered that he was infested with lice. I was shaking louse powder over him from a canister when a customer arrived in the yard. He watched me through a cloud of DDT for a few minutes, then asked me what I was doing. Thinking that a silly question deserved a silly answer, I said, 'I'm shaking fertilizer on him to make him grow.'

'You're wasting your time,' said the buyer. 'It couldn't possibly work.' Poor Castaway was one of the thinnest horses I've ever seen. I bought him cheaply, the 'sweetener' in a bunch of four. I was lucky, as he soon filled out on good grass (the bicycle-fattening variety) and went to the Metropolitan Police.

In the dreadful winter of 1962/63, even well-off people had a job to keep condition on their animals. Hay wasn't merely dear, it was unobtainable. Oats couldn't be bought except at a crazy price. Undernourished foals and yearlings began to appear in the cattle fairs, brought from the West by lorry.

I bought a grey yearling, rising two, for £25, hardly knowing if he was a horse or a pony in the making. He was named Hungry Hill after the place of his birth in the Arra Mountains. The old man I bought him from took the money and went to ground in the nearest pub, but I winkled him out and he agreed to lead the colt home. Hours passed and he hadn't arrived. I set out on a bike to look for him. Rounding a corner, about a mile from home, I met the old man, plodding along, halter rope in hand. It was a long rope, and the halter was trailing along the road at the end of it. There was no sign of Hungry Hill, and I found him nibbling briars a long way back. As for the old man, having found the horse it seemed I'd lost the seller. However, passing the Thatched Cottage Inn, I noticed a halter lying outside. A rope attached to it led under the door into the Select Bar.

That winter, some non-horsey friends of mine took pity on a tinkers' pony and bought it for their little boy. It was quiet to ride, but even when the grass came it was thin and weak. They asked me to have a look at it. I did. It was a miserable little dun, its mane and tail clipped right off, apparently with a blunt knife. Its tiny feet made me wonder, and I examined its teeth. I'd been told it was five years old, but no, it was a yearling. It was also an entire colt. These facts came as a shock to the owners, who optimistically went in search of the tinker they had bought it from. They searched in vain. It was just as well; the pony grew into a cob, keeping pace with the growth of his child rider for years.

*

At last the tide turned, I began to relax. I was able to afford to reclaim all the low-lying part of the farm and to stock it with cattle; I bought a new car, upped the turnover of horses, replaced the tractor and took two-weeks holiday in England every summer. I got commissions to buy police horses and troopers in half dozens rather than singly, I bought hunters for private customers as well as unbroken stock and potential showjumpers.

When coaching marathons became popular, I got orders for matched pairs, usually of Irish draught type or, much more difficult, requests to buy something to match a horse in a poor-quality colour snapshot. Suddenly there was a craze for having everything matching. I think Laura Ashley may have had something to do with it. As rooms blossomed with matching chintzes on every piece of furniture with the motif repeated on the wallpaper, the fashion spread to co-ordinated dressing and, for those who were interested, to matched pairs, or teams, of horses. Those who couldn't afford such things contented themselves with buying spotted, odd-coloured, or in any way eye-catching mounts.

The horse world is full of old proverbs, many of which are non-sense. One of these is, 'A good horse is never a bad colour.' The saying probably referred originally to piebalds, skewbalds and Appaloosas, which are now highly prized. Any of these is preferable to a washy colour, although owners have ways of getting round it. Washy chestnuts are described as 'Palomino' and washy browns as 'dark dun' when they are for sale.

[145]

In my long association with horses, I have learned to connect certain colours with characteristics. A washy colour may go with a wimpish temperament, and a bright colour with an excitable nature. As for markings, we all know the old rhyme about white socks:

> One – buy him,
> Two – try him,
> Three – suspect him,
> Four – reject him.

Another version turns this one upside down:

> One white sock, keep him not a day,
> Two white socks, send him far away,
> Three white socks, sell him to a friend,
> Four white socks, keep him to the end.

When horses were more plentiful, it was difficult to sell one with white 'stockings' above the knee. I knew a man, I'll call him Tom, who owned a chestnut, a big handsome gelding, with one foreleg white almost to the elbow. The horse was to be sold at a fair, and Tom bought a bottle of hair dye in a shade called 'Autumn Glow'. The colour, as shown on the packet, exactly matched the horse.

Tom went to a lot of trouble. He bandaged the fetlock down to the hoof so as to leave a convincing 'sock' and soaked the rest in dye. It dried out a cruel shade of egg-yolk yellow. Tom applied more dye and the leg turned bright orange with a faint tinge of green. It was then that Tom thought better of it, and tried to wash the dye out. 'Up to six shampoos,' said the instructions. About eight shampoos later the leg was back to the egg-yolk colour. At that stage, I bought the horse myself and turned him out to fade. Months later, the leg was still yellowish, but he was a good horse and made money. He won working hunter classes under the name Autumn Glow.

The prejudice against chestnuts, especially mares, is deeply rooted, although it is the second commonest colour after bay. It is also dominant, chestnut parents being obliged to produce chestnut foals, whether they want to or not.

I have owned scores of chestnut mares, including two absolute devils. Why they didn't kill me between them I shall never know. I have also owned dozens which were as quiet as wood. This phrase, 'as quiet as wood', reminds me of a less apt metaphor, 'as quiet as a lamb'. A quiet lamb is probably ill. A dealer I know has another simile, 'as gentle as a bee'. After my experience with Paul and the hayrake, this sounds to me like a joke in poor taste.

The saying applied to Prophetic, 'A black horse with sorra a white hair will kill seven men,' I have found, if not literally true, to have some foundation. I have never known a horse that was black all over which didn't have a flawed character. Sulkiness is often the problem rather than real badness. Black is not a popular colour (outside the Household Cavalry) nor yet a usual one. Yet the equine heroes of fiction are frequently black or, equally uncommon, white. Black Beauty and Black Bess are obvious examples of the first, while damsels in distress were rescued by knights riding white stallions – not chestnut mares.

I wouldn't buy a piebald for myself, but a certain lady had a fancy for one and offered a fancy price to match. She wasn't worried about performance, but only colour and reasonable looks. Accordingly, I bought a pretty piebald mare, only to find that my customer had changed her mind.

The mare, like the lady, had a temperament. She looked attractive (the mare, I mean) and had two paces, a walk and a slowish gallop. She didn't believe in jumping and was slow in the uptake except when crossing a muddy gap. Then, she would drop as if shot and roll. Most coloured horses have pony blood, and rolling in gateways is a pony's trick. In the case of a piebald or skewbald, there may be a protective instinct to camouflage the white patches. I have found light greys far dirtier in their stables than bays or browns – they need too much grooming for my taste.

Some horse, keep themselves scrupulously clean; others do not. I will refrain from further human comparisons.

The dirtiest horse I ever owned was Lily. This oddly named mare was cream-coloured and had to be washed all over every time she was ridden. In addition to normal ways of getting filthy, she would wriggle out of her rugs and lie down in the wettest places she could find.

When I sold her, Lily was renamed Cornflakes. They say that it's unlucky to change a horse's name, which was the reason I had not done so. Lily/Cornflakes brought no luck to anybody.

*

One of the more pleasant aspects of dealing in the sixties was that it was then that the meat trade began to fall off. No longer was a three-year-old's value reckoned by what he weighed. No longer were good Irish draught mares sent to the factory the first time they missed being in foal. Right up to the early seventies, when prices rose steeply, a smallish, unbroken filly was worth more for the meat trade than anything else.

In earlier times I had bought many a horse which would otherwise never have had a chance to prove his worth. Some dealers bought only animals which had been salvaged from lorry-loads of 'killers', getting an even number of bargains and duds. I remember seeing a nice little horse about 15.1 hands being led on to a shipper's lorry at Cahirmee fair. I was suspicious because he had been clipped out, and let him go. Another, less cynical customer liked him and gave profit – he was still costing only £60. The lorry departed, and the buyer told everybody about his bargain. Another customer got interested, said he might give profit. They took the horse into the barrack field to canter him, and he dropped dead almost at once. The boastful buyer was left with nothing but a body to dispose of.

I have bought a few off the lorries myself, usually unbroken Irish draught types with size, suitable for police work. One of my favourites was also one of my first bargains – Mona by name. I was in Nenagh, buying cattle in the square, when I saw a sad-looking bunch of horses being loaded for the boat. I knew the dealer who had bought them locally, and he invited me to 'Pick where you like for £35.' On closer inspection, they weren't a brilliant lot, but I sorted out a nice type of five-year-old grey mare, about 15.3 hands.

Mona was well made and not common; only one feature hinted at humble origins. On her upper lip, she wore a small white moustache which grew sideways from a centre parting. I hastily clipped it off.

Mona had been broken and gone in harness. She had a perfect mouth, a lovely nature and was as sound as a bell. Even my mother enjoyed riding her.

I sold Mona for double her cost and still cheap to a dealer from Yorkshire. He passed her on to Rowley Harker, for many years master of the Jedforest Hunt. The dealer reported this sale on the phone to a friend. As he was sparing with his aitches, dealer number two thought he'd said, 'Marjorie's grey mare's gone to Rollearca.' So he rang me up and told me that Mona had been retired to stud and covered by a son of Nearco. That's how rumours start – not that I believed him. Years later, Rowley Harker sent me a photograph of himself and Mona, saying he'd hunted hounds off her for many seasons and wanted another. 'Preferably clean shaven,' he added.

Another horse of mine which was lucky to survive, was my only purchase as Goff's Bloodstock Sales. A dark bay thoroughbred filly, she looked like the makings of a show pony. She cost fifty-five guineas, and the underbidder was a dogfood man. Piccolina hadn't the temperament for showing, being a wild, scatterbrained creature. She also grew too big, which meant she was the dealers' nightmare, an undersized misfit – and a misfit with a cold back, at that. I sold this one after six strenuous months. She was more or less rideable, and might have made a polo pony had she been less nervous. Unfortunately, she wasn't up to the weight of anyone strong enough to control her. I sold her for £85 (a huge loss in real terms) and didn't expect to hear anything good about her. Wrong again. Piccolina found her true vocation in life and won fourteen pony races at Northolt Park.

*

Not long after I sold Piccolina, horses changed my life. I was lying in bed with a bad go of 'flu, when a friend of mine called, saying he wanted to borrow one of my horses for an Englishman to go hunting on. 'He can borrow one from somebody else,' I said fretfully. 'Why should I lend my horse to some ham-fisted tourist? Is he any good on a horse?'

'Good? Of course he is. Johnny Quarton goes like a pigeon across country. No nerves at all – nice fellow too.'

'I don't care how nice he is. He's not getting one of my young horses – he'd knock it up.'

'But I told him you'd lend him Vicky. I could bring him up to see you if you like.'

'I don't like, and you shouldn't have told him anything of the kind. Do go away – I'm dying.' The Englishman borrowed from somebody more charitable, and I missed meeting my future husband. It was years before he returned to Ireland.

*

Around the time when I refused to lend John Quarton a horse, a field adjoining my farm was let to an elderly farmer who kept a dozen bullocks in it. This was a nuisance, as the field was landlocked, and I had to let him drive his cattle across my land. (Eventually, I bought the field myself.) The farmer, Mick Doheny, owned a black-brown mare which he turned in the field to fatten her up. He reckoned she would fetch £60 for beef.

The mare might have fattened faster if she hadn't persisted in jumping the boundary fence and joining my horses. It seemed a pity to allow such a good natural jumper to go for beef, so I bought her for £60. I tried to sell her to the Household Cavalry, but she wasn't black enough. Then, as no other customers turned up, I passed her on to a Yorkshire dealer who sold her for £80 to John Quarton, who hunted with the Middleton and the Sinnington Hounds in Yorkshire.

John hunted the mare, which was called Amazon, and she was a brilliant performer. At the end of the season, he sold her to the field master, Sir William Brooksbank, for £350. Money for old rope, thought John, and asked the dealer to buy him another horse from the same farm. I got a phone call from the dealer who'd bought Amazon, not saying who his customer was, just that he wanted a decent three-year-old gelding and had a preference for a grey.

I went to the next fair, which was at Thurles, and soon spotted what looked like a suitable horse. I feared he might be expensive, as he was turned out as if he was going to a show. He wore a bridle with gleaming brass buckles, no saddle, and was being led about by a monk in a habit and sandals.

I was a bit shy of doing business with a monk, although I knew that his monastery, Mount St Joseph, near Roscrea, was famous for its livestock. The monk was called Brother Lazarian, and it was impossible to deal with him. He'd been told the least he could take and it was too much. 'I trained the colt myself, he has a great mouth,' he said, and with that, he kilted up his habit and vaulted onto its bare back. He trotted up and down the street and offered to take the grey over jumps if I could find any. It was no good, we both had a price limit. However, I agreed to go to the monastery and haggle with Brother Lazarian's superior.

I did this, driving up to the main door which stood open and walking in. At once, a group of monks rushed at me and drove me out with shooing movements, shutting the doors, which they leant against as if I might attempt to force my way in. 'No women allowed in here,' one of them gasped in a tone of horror. Feeling guilty and ashamed, I allowed myself to be led away to the farmyard.

I was still unable to give the monks' price and they sold the grey elsewhere. Then my dealer upped his price and I was able to give the new owner a bit of profit and get some myself. John got the horse and it was almost as lucky as Amazon.

After this, John fell out with our go-between and came to Ireland to do his own horse-trading. (He'd been led to believe that M. Smithwick was a man, and got a considerable shock when we met.) Not long afterwards, he decided to stay. 'If you can't beat 'em, join 'em,' he said. If Amazon had found her way to some French dinner-table, my life would have been very different.

*

Marriage had not been high on my list of priorities. I was undomesticated and unmaternal to a degree. I was indeed fortunate in getting not only a wonderful husband, but a ready-made family of seven as well. I produced one daughter of my own with reasonable efficiency, and adapted to a new lifestyle with ease.

Women move house more often than not when they marry, but I was fortunate. It was John who left home and moved to Ireland. From the moment he arrived, it seemed as if he'd always lived here. Impossible to imagine Crannagh without him. I'd been dealing with Yorkshire people for many years and loved staying in North Yorkshire, where John lived, a beautiful place and not unlike parts of Tipperary.

There is a stage Yorkshireman, just as there is a stage Irishman. Both stereotypes have a tiny core of fact. John was the exact opposite of the popular idea, being warm-hearted, generous and rather emotional, characteristics more typical of Ireland, which is probably why he made his home here so happily. He'd a sense of humour very much on the same wavelength as my own, and his outlook on life was so youthful that the difference in our ages was never a problem.

When John left Yorkshire, he turned over his farm to his son Robert, who was only twenty-two. Robert took it on along with the care of his two youngest sisters, and if he minded he never showed it. It is really remarkable that two people as thoroughly anchored by dependants and property as we were ever managed to compromise our way to a happy marriage. We did, and were inseparable for seventeen years.

My wedding day sticks in my mind for other reasons besides the conventional ones. I refused, much to my mother's annoyance, to wear white or have a bevy of bridesmaids. I compromised by going to a hairdresser for the first time in my life. As I also took the milk to the Creamery and the service was at 11 a.m, good timing was needed. As I drove to Nenagh at seventy miles an hour, a cow wandered out of a gateway on to the road. Forced to drive behind her (in front would have been fatal for both of us), I just grazed her backside with my wing mirror as she suddenly decided to reverse. The other wing mirror touched the nose of another cow following behind. No harm done, but I arrived at the Creamery suffering from more than wedding nerves.

Later, duly curled and waved, I waited on my cousin's arm to walk up the isle. I was to do this to the strains of the hymn 'Lead us,

Heavenly Father, lead us'. My cousin, another John, knowing my general vagueness, and not at all surprised when I was late, hissed at me, 'When the choir gets to the words, "keenest woe", we go in. Left, right … keep in step with me.' Almost overcome with a fit of the giggles, I did as I was told.

*

I carried on with horse-dealing almost without a break. I don't recommend buying a bunch of troopers in a busy fair when seven months pregnant, nor yet trying to carry on all business from the car because the baby's in a carry-cot in the back; but both can be and were done. We were immensely happy.

From then on, the horse-dealing remained mainly my concern, as did the buying and selling of cattle. John turned to tillage and sheep, and, the only interest we didn't already share, Border Collie dogs.

CHAPTER EIGHTEEN

Guinea-men and Old Men

John wasn't entirely unprepared when he came to live in Ireland. He'd been spending as much time as he could here, and we'd been to several fairs together. At the first, Limerick, he got bored and wandered away, to be accosted by one of the guinea-hunters with whom the fairs abounded. My own helper, Fairo, came dashing to warn me. 'Miss Smithwick, quick! There's a tangler talking to your pigeon.' Poor John.

It was at Kilrush that I met Fairo. Anyone at a fair intending to buy more than one horse had to have a helper. You cannot buy two horses at once, so you had to hand over each as he was bought to your helper, and go in search of another, thus saving time. There were various grades of assistance available. At the top was the person capable of buying but perhaps lacking the cash or the market, who would do everything for his boss except sign the cheques. He would be working on a generous and fixed commission. At the other end of the scale were the guinea-men or tanglers, whose aim was to earn a few shillings, or preferably pounds, by 'making a deal'. They seldom did any actual work. They would appear when a deal was imminent, shouting, 'Give the horse.' 'What's between you?' 'Let you divide the tenner,' and so on. The deal done, they would collect (from both sides if possible, known as 'touching both ways'), and instantly disappear.

Fairo came about halfway between these extremes. A small man with a stick taller than himself, he was utterly honest and dependable. He only helped to make a deal when asked. He took my horses to have their hind shoes taken off, got halters, unplaited manes and dressed manes and tails with Jeyes' Fluid. Then he would load the horses. I trusted him absolutely. He attended every big fair provided it wasn't on a Thursday, when he was a drover at Ennis Mart. I thought for some time that he was called Pharaoh, and even named a horse after him, but I was wrong.

There is a convention in buying horses in the streets. You can stop a man riding or leading one, ask him for details, including the price, and ask to have the animal run out and back in order to judge its action. After this, you might make a bid for it. It would be up to you to make a deal without allowing the owner to take his horse away. Once out of shouting distance, or if you turned your back, another dealer could cut in. Not before. One day in Kilrush I was buying a likely Swiss trooper and the owner trotted her out for me. When he'd gone far enough, I shouted, 'That'll do, bring her back.' I'd bid £200 already. As the man turned his horse, a guinea-man I knew by sight stepped out of the crowd and spoke to him. I couldn't hear what was said, but I was fairly sure he was passing on a higher bid. The owner of the mare just kept going with her until the crowd hid them from view. Fairo rushed off and came back in a frightful temper. The guinea hunter's boss was paying for the mare. Every unwritten law had been broken. 'There's nothing to be done,' I said.

'I could organize some discipline,' said Fairo. I'm sorry to say that I laughed. I went off to the café for a sandwich.

The café was a long narrow room with tables all down one side. Only the one at the far end was vacant. I was doing away with the sandwiches when there was a commotion at the door and Fairo appeared, standing very erect. Then he came marching down the café, followed by the erring guinea-man who was being led, not gently, by two heavies whom I knew by sight. Right down the long room they came, and Fairo stopped at my table. 'This man wants to say he's sorry,' he proclaimed. The heavies gave the offender a hard shake and he muttered something. I muttered something too. I was almost overcome by an unseemly fit of giggles. Then the procession turned round and went out, with Fairo bringing up the rear. The discipline must have worked. Nobody ever, at any fair, tried that particular trick on me again.

When I introduced Fairo to John, and told him we were getting married, he was delighted. 'I try to take care of her,' he told John, 'but it isn't easy.'

*

Nothing in my life was easy. Actually buying horses I could sell was often easier than getting myself to the fair and getting my purchases home.

I often grumbled about inadequate transport, but many people carried on thriving businesses or ran successful farms without a car. They depended on lifts, and it was normal for those who had cars to fill them with people who hadn't. I learned early that it was inadvisable to give lifts to farmers on the way home from fairs, as they were usually half-jarred. Today, a woman on her own would be worried about mugging or even rape; then, one's only difficulty was to dislodge the passenger from the car without actually taking him home. But it's hard to leave an elderly man on the side of the road on a chilly winter's day, even if he does seem to be somewhat under the weather.

I was heading home after a long and unprofitable day at Newmarket fair in North Cork. 'Are you going far?' I asked.

'That depends on yourself.' My passenger lit a large and smelly pipe. 'I'll travel as far as I'm carried. I like to travel.' His tone was aggressive. I shut up.

After a time, I remarked, 'There were some beautiful foals at Newmarket today.'

The man turned his head and glared at me through a cloud of smoke. 'Horses aren't beautiful,' he said at last. 'If you think they are, you have no eye for beauty.' He puffed at his pipe for a bit and then said, 'But then, not many has the true eye.'

'You have it, I suppose,' I said sarcastically.

'Oh aye. I have it all right.' He smoked in silence for a minute or two. 'What beauty,' he demanded suddenly, 'is there in skin and flesh and blood and bones? Horses! Women! They can change any time. Do you dare to deny it?' I didn't dare.

I was driving into Charleville as he spoke, and offered to set him down there. 'No, there's men in Charleville that don't like me. Take me to Limerick.' Hoping that the men of Limerick would be more tolerant, I drove on.

I thought he'd gone to sleep – the pipe had gone out and his chin was on his chest. But suddenly he startled me by shouting, 'Stop here!' We were on open road, not far from Croom. A stark white bungalow stood at the roadside, surrounded by spiked railings. It was so new that the grass hadn't grown over the builder's rubble. The railings were painted cobalt blue with silver spikes. My passenger sat up and pointed with his pipe. 'Talk about beauty,' he cried. 'That's the real apple. If you have an eye for beauty like me, you can't be happy under thatch. It's in slates and cement and good hard-wearing paint that you see it.'

'Is this where you live? Will I put you down here?'

'Oh, you're in a big hurry to get rid of me. If you listen to me, my dear woman, you might learn something.' I managed not to suggest that he might learn some manners, and set him down thankfully just outside Limerick at a pub (slated, and painted emerald green picked out in pink.)

I steadfastly refused to give lifts for weeks afterwards.

*

Years later, when I was as much interested in buying a good sheepdog as a good horse, I was driving with John along a mountain road. We were heading for a farm where, we had heard, there was a useful young dog for sale.

The day was unpleasant as only a December afternoon can be in the mountains. There was sleet in the rain and a promise of snow to come. There were no houses, no signposts, no villages. We were lost.

When we overtook an old man plodding along with a bundle on

his back, we hailed him with all the enthusiasm of Good King Wenceslas. We asked him the way to Jim Daly's house (not his real name), and he answered, 'Aren't I going there myself?'

Delighted, I opened the door and helped him to stow his bundle on the back seat. 'A few little things people gave me for the Christmas,' said the old man, who told us his name was Jerry. 'The times are gone to hell, but most give me a tin of biscuits or a few fags,' he added.

As we drove along, Jerry entertained us with anecdotes, mostly scandalous, and pointed out places where people had been killed. 'Is it much farther?' John asked.

'It isn't. You can stop here, at this farm.' We stopped, and Jerry hurried into the house. Thinking he must have business with Jim Daly, we waited … and waited. At last, I went to the door and saw three or four people sitting in front of the fire, drinking. 'Come on in, the two of you and have a jar,' Jerry invited largely. We inquired which was Jim Daly.

This isn't Daly's at all,' said Jerry. 'I made a mistake. Sit down and take a drink when it's offered you. Isn't it going on Christmas?'

We accepted hot whiskey and lemonade – heavy on whiskey, light on lemonade – but refused to wait for more. Back in the car, we again asked Jerry to tell us the way to Jim Daly's. 'What hurry is on you?' he replied. 'Sure we'll be a long time dead.' A mile or so further on, we reached a house where Jerry said he had to call 'for a minute'. We waited ten minutes, then blew the horn. Jerry appeared, wiping his mouth. 'Take it easy, will you,' he said. 'You couldn't get away from that woman, she's the biggest gabber from hell to Bedlam.'

'If you won't take us to Jim Daly's, you can get out and walk.'

'Walk? Where's your Christian charity, missis? And I near eighty years of age and the season that's in it. Stop here at this cottage.'

'Is it Daly's?'

'It is not, but the woman of the house buried her husband lately. We'll get a few drinks if we play our cards right.' We let him out of the car, telling him to get his few drinks and a lift home while he was at it.

I'd spotted a village in the distance, and there we asked our way.

We were wrong by ten miles and had to go back the way we had come, arriving at Jim Daly's as the light faded. It dawned on us that Daly's was the last farm we'd passed before we overtook Jerry, and furthermore, that Jerry had recently left the Daly farm well warmed with Christmas cheer.

It was, of course, a wasted journey, as you can't watch a dog working sheep in the dusk. He looked a nice sort and we agreed to return. Jim invited us in for a cup of tea. 'I'd offer you whiskey,' he said, 'but Jerry emptied the bottle on me – he makes his rounds every year. He'll be legless by now, but he finds his way home like a cat.'

It was cosy in the kitchen, but outside, the rain streamed down harder than ever. The couple from the next farm arrived and fresh tea was brewed. We agreed that it was a terrible night for an old man to be out walking, and that we must look out for Jerry on the way home. He might have passed out on the side of the road.

He hadn't. When we left, we found him asleep in the back of our car. Woken up, none too gently, by John, he had no difficulty in directing us to his own house, which was about another five miles out of our way.

*

Some time after this, we got a late-night call from a farmer we knew well who was stranded in the village of Hollyford with a pick-up full of calves and a broken axle. We were happy to help, as this man had helped us when we'd been stranded in the middle of nowhere. Hollyford is twenty miles away on a mountainous road, and it was 11 p.m. when we reached it.

'It's not just a matter of getting the calves home,' said our friend. 'I can leave them till tomorrow. But I've an old man in the pick-up who asked for a lift this morning. He's been cadging drinks all day, now he's paralytic and I don't know where he lives.' I wasn't greatly surprised when I looked through the window and saw Jerry, sleeping like a baby.

'I know exactly where he lives,' I said. 'It's not on your road home, or ours.' We transferred the old man to our car and took first him, then the farmer home. Jerry didn't wake when we hauled him out of the pick-up and into the car. In fact he never stirred until we reached his home. I was in the back with him, the two men in the front. 'Wake up, Jerry,' I said, 'you're home.'

Jerry sat up and yawned. He didn't seem particularly surprised to find himself in a different car with a different driver. He climbed out of the car, staggered a little, then turned and shook my hand. 'You know, missis, I like you,' he said. 'Give me a shout the next time you're travelling and I'll come along for the spin.'

*

Many readers will have noticed how often I had problems dealing with difficult old men. There was always a good supply of these in the fairs, where they were useful to dodgy dealers for showing 'travellers'. Travellers were unsound or unrideable horses which travelled from fair to fair. Their market value was decided by the meat trade, but their appearance suggested a much higher price.

The dealer, finding himself stuck with a good-looking horse with an incurable fault, would turn him out to grass and let his mane and tail grow, then get an accomplice, usually old and hard up, to show him in the fair as unbroken.

The word went round rapidly when a traveller appeared on the scene; regular buyers got to know them. I remember seeing the same one at every fair from May to November. I very nearly bought one myself in Spancilhill, only being saved by Fairo at the last moment.

The old men selling travellers never knew anything. The conversation ran along well-worn lines. 'How old is he?'

'I forget. Look at his teeth.'

'How much?' (The reply would be much less than the animal's looks suggested, about four times his real value.)

'How's he bred?'

'I don't know, I'm selling him for the brother.'

'Where's your brother, then?'

'He's in America. I know nothing about horses.' This was the point where the fools rushed in. The canny, at the first mention of a brother in America or a nephew in England or a son in Australia, would turn away.

Sometimes an innocent old man selling honestly was unable to deal, because his horse was thought to be a traveller. At one of my first fairs, I stopped a toothless old man leading a bay mare and asked the usual questions. He was stone deaf, so I had to shout.

'What age is she?' No reply. 'How old is she?' I yelled. There was no glimmer of understanding in the old man's eye. 'CAN I LOOK AT HER TEETH?'

The old man looked at me in surprise. 'No teesh, no teesh,' he said, opening his mouth wide so that I could see.

Much embarrassed, especially as the usual interested crowd was collecting, I persisted. 'HOW MUCH?' I screamed. He got that and named a price. £100.

'Has she been ridden?'

'Moycarkey,' said the old man.

'HAS SHE BEEN RIDDEN?'

'Moycarkey.'

Completely baffled, I looked round for enlightenment. 'It's where he lives,' said a voice in the crowd. I gave up and left the field to a man who fanned out four £10 notes under the old man's nose, pressed them into his hand and led the mare away. The mare wasn't a traveller. The toothless one genuinely had a brother in the States. There was trouble, I heard afterwards.

*

An old man in another league altogether was Billy Bamlet from Yorkshire, with whom I dealt for many years. He was over ninety when he died in 1985, and was seventy-five when I sold him the showjumper Buttevant Boy. I had shown the horse to Billy with the police in mind, and he turned him down because he was only 15.3 hands, so I kept him for the summer and broke him in. He was so quiet, he almost broke himself in. I lunged him over a pole and was impressed by his careful jumping, but I don't pretend to have recognized his potential. I only sat on him a couple of times. He was destined to carry a policeman in London. Why bother?

That autumn, Billy returned and bought the horse, but he was turned down by the police for a bump on the hock. Graham Fletcher had reason to be devoutly thankful for this. That year, Billy Bamlet hunted the three-year-old regularly, giving Graham Fletcher's father, Ken, a lead over a formidable set of park rails. Before they went home, Billy had sold Ken a half share in the horse for £200.

Buttevant Boy's jumping career spanned more than twelve years, starting in the Young Riders' event at Wembley, when his age and Graham's added up to just twenty-one. He won the Grand Prix at Aachen and at Dublin. At the end of his career, he divided the Grand Prix at Arena North with David Broome. In between he won steadily at the top shows, never being lame or off form. He was placed twice in the Hickstead Derby, being one of the first to jump a double clear there, and was shortlisted for the Olympics three times.

I have had many other top-class jumpers through my hands, but Buttevant Boy must surely have been the best. The trouble was that one was at the mercy of the people one sold to. They didn't have to tell you that your horse was winning all around him if they didn't want to.

When Buttevant Boy was in his heyday, I was besieged by people offering to sell me his brothers, sisters, uncles and aunts. Every one I looked at was as good as Buttevant Boy – or would be. I got tired of hearing on the radio and reading in magazines that he came from Buttevant. He was never near it. Billy named him after a jumping horse he'd had pre-war.

Of course, Billy was anxious to buy 'another Buttevant Boy', and we went to Buttevant itself looking for something with potential. 'Can he jump?' Billy asked a man leading a smart sort of grey.

'Jump? He can lep like a Cork flea.' I bought that one myself and passed him on to Billy later. Named Billy B by his next owner, he was a big winner showjumping and a great advertisement for the fleas of Cork.

The same day, we were looking at a heavy bay, which might, when trimmed, have suited one of the less fussy police forces. Billy had a harness job in mind. The bay's owner, insulted, said, 'Don't waste him in harness. You'd easy teach him to jump a gate if you had him.'

Billy answered, 'It'd be a lot easier to teach him to lift the latch with his teeth.' I think he was right.

Then there was Mr Liar. Billy was with me when I bought Mr Liar. He was a big, handsome horse, but on the strong side. 'He'll carry a lot of weight,' said the owner.

'Pull a lot,' said Bill. 'And I bet I could run faster and jump higher.' (Billy was short, fat and in his late seventies.)

Aggressively, the owner asked, 'What would you say if I told you I'd seen him clear six feet?'

'I'd say you was a bloody liar,' said Billy.

Mr Liar went to the Hull police and presumably didn't have to clear six feet. I changed his name to Tall Story when I sold him, but he is entered in my books as Mr Liar.

Another horse with an unusual name was called Daddy. This grey gelding took a lot of buying. John and I visited the farm again and again while the owner dithered. First he'd sell, then he wouldn't. At last, John told him we were sick of this carry-on. He could make up his mind or keep his horse. The man, fortyish, married with a family and a salaried job, said, 'I'll have to ask Daddy.'

Daddy lived elsewhere, so we had to wait while our man telephoned him. Daddy consented to the sale of the horse. We bought him. I said, 'I didn't know your father owned the horse, you should have told us earlier.'

'He doesn't own him, I do. But I like the advice of an older person when I'm selling.'

CHAPTER NINETEEN

Some Sharp Customers

Life in the seventies was wonderful. Everything was going our way, it seemed. The farm flourished, so did the dogs, and the horse trade was on the way up.

Mind you, I was lucky that I was not a widow. My wedding present to John had been a three-year-old horse, chosen more for his looks and his jumping ability than his temperament. He was a horse I couldn't have afforded if there hadn't been an 'if'. There were two 'ifs'. One was a cold back, no matter how often he was ridden, the other was a slightly overshot jaw. Because of this, John called him 'Goose Neb' – I've forgotten his real name.

John and Goose Neb got on fine until one day when the horse caught his rider off guard – searching for a handkerchief. A moment later, a sky-high buck sent John crashing down on the cobbled yard. By the time he'd recovered from a fractured pelvis, I'd managed to sell the horse, which made an eventer for some reckless rider.

Goose Neb wasn't the only sharp customer I wished on poor John. Before we were married, there was Clancy, illegitimate offspring of a thoroughbred yearling and a pony. He was as hard as nails and as slippery as an eel; a brilliant performer and what hopeful sellers call 'an interesting ride'. Although I never fell off him, it was a near thing once or twice.

I remember taking him to a meet of the hounds which took place in Banbha Square in Nenagh, at a time when he should still have been in breaking tackle. When I tried to restrain his caperings, he ran backwards up the steps of the Provincial Bank, now the Garda barracks, and bumped the swing doors open with his bottom. He then backed into the entrance hall, off the weathered stone and on to the polished Victorian tiles where he slithered wildly.

As I wasn't on the friendliest of terms with my bank manager at the time, I thought it prudent to dismount and lead Clancy back down the steps. Somebody took rather a good picture of this, but I felt deeply humiliated. John got Clancy a few months later, and never had any trouble with him. Not so the foxhunting Yorkshire family who got him next; the brains of a pony allied to the strength of a horse make a formidable combination. Although his mother was a quiet little thing and his father a racehorse, Clancy was solid pony, through and through. He could not only lift a latch, but could and did slide back a bolt with his teeth. At a major agricultural show (where he won two prizes) he got loose and found his way into the refreshment tent. There, so I was told, he ate several bunches of flowers and a plateful of egg sandwiches.

Why is it that someone is invariably present with a camera when one is being publicly made a fool of? Why can't they be there when they might be appreciated? Another occasion which was immortalized in Banbha Square was the only time I can remember falling off a horse when it was actually standing still. This occurred at a holiday meet, in the middle of an interested crowd and under the nose of a photographer. The horse in question was called Timothy, a tall, narrow – very narrow – bay three-year-old. Riding him was rather like being astride a clothes line but, although dreadfully green, he was reasonably quiet.

What I didn't know about Timothy was that he had the trick of blowing himself out when his girths were being tightened. Only grass-fed ponies do this as a rule. I suppose I mounted when he was holding his breath and forgot to check my girths. Anyway, in the middle of the crowded square, he breathed out, gave a convulsive wriggle and somehow shot his saddle back almost to his loins. Both

I and the saddle finished up underneath him, and it was lucky that he didn't seem disturbed by this, merely turning his head to peer at me in some surprise. Timothy was out of a pony mare, I discovered afterwards.

I've never dealt in ponies for choice. The average pony gives more trouble than two horses and makes little profit. The pity is that they go for children to ride, so you have to be very sure they are suitable. I have always been tall and heavy, and a pony which thought it wise to be on his best behaviour with me could show a different side of his nature to a child. Having started on big horses, my faith in equine nature was complete – it took a pony to shake it. It's a great pity that so many of them have a bit of the devil in them, as they give most people their first experience of horses.

Many years ago, when I was going to Kilrush fair, a friend asked me to buy a small, cheap pony to pull a trap to amuse the children. I wandered about looking for anything that was attractive, dog quiet, small and cheap. At last I found what I wanted, with the tinkers.

The episode started badly and went on worse. The pony was a prettily marked piebald with a small head. A boy of about eight was riding him up the street. When I walked into the road to stop him, the child shouted, 'Don't you frighten my bloody horse!' However, his father appeared and told him to shut his gob. I went to the modest limit I'd been given and bought the pony. Father wandered off, leaving the boy in charge, gob still shut.

'Nice little pony,' I said, 'Is he part Connemara?'

'No,' said the boy, 'I think he's a Friesian. Give me the cash,' he added, 'and you can take him away and boil him if you like.'

'I'll give you a cheque,' I said. I didn't fancy giving cash to this particular eight-year-old. I'd have put nothing past him.

'My Da won't take no bloody cheques,' said the child. I was wasting time on a non-profit-making deal, so I asked Fairo to take the pony to the lorry and told the boy I'd see his father later. I walked off, leaving Fairo to deal with him.

Later, I was having a meal in the packed dining-room of the hotel when the boy and his father appeared in the doorway of the restaurant. 'That's her, Da!' shouted the child, pointing.

With that, the tinker marched in, complete with slouch hat, red neckerchief and whip. He strode up to my table. 'I want to be paid!' he declared, in ringing tones. There was total silence, as everyone in the room stopped eating to stare while I found the money. I met this tinker again, many times, and he always tried to sell me something. 'Remember we dealt before, lady.' I did remember.

*

Am I giving the impression that I bought only in the fairs? I didn't; about half my horses were bought off the land.

Even today, buying off a farm is more expensive than waiting for a fair or sale. But it was, and is, the only thing to do if you need to secure a particular animal and daren't risk opposition.

In my early days, lack of a car obliged me to deal locally, at farms which were in reach of my bike. Some of the owners I met were great people to deal with, but sometimes I started a family feud when I wanted to buy a horse. One member would be keen to sell, another determined not to. Another would think – correctly – that if I was offering £50 and expecting profit, a private buyer would give more.

I remember a household consisting of an old brother and two old sisters. The brother, Denis, had told me he had a horse to sell. I went to the farm, and met him cycling down the laneway to meet me. 'You'll have to ask the sisters will they sell,' he said.

'You ask them,' I suggested.

'I will not,' Denis said. 'They're devils on wheels. You deal with them. Talk to Julia – she's the boss.'

Looking past him, I saw two elderly women standing, arms folded, outside the house. 'Which is Julia?' I asked nervously.

'Ah, you couldn't mistake Julia,' said her brother. 'You could wipe poison off her face.' With that, he grabbed his bike and pedalled off as fast as he could, probably to the nearest pub.

My nerve almost failed me – he was right about Julia – I was glad when the horse turned out to be unsuitable. Years later, the same family was selling a daughter of this mare (which they had never managed to sell). I told John the above story and he laughed at me.

'I'll deal with Julia,' he said confidently.

I told him to go ahead, and refused to go along and see fair play. He returned routed, and the filly, like its mother, stayed where it was.

*

A farmer with only one horse to sell would often overvalue it, certain that his goose was a swan. Especially deluded were two brothers, well up in their seventies, who were semi-retired. They had let most of their land and sold most of their stock. They retained two cows and a horse.

The horse, a quality bay gelding, was seven years old. The brothers had bred him and lovingly watched him grow into a nice sort of lightweight. He was not exceptional, not a show horse, but there would be no difficulty in selling such an animal. The problem was that, in all his seven years, he had never been haltered except, presumably, when he was castrated.

The hair-raising price asked left me speechless. The old men evidently thought they owned another Arkle. I explained that, even if I could have afforded him, their horse would be aware of his own strength. He would take a lot of breaking in. The old men listened pityingly and offered me a cup of tea.

Some weeks later, a well-heeled customer from England came to my farm and bought a 'made' hunter. He showed me a list of several animals he had been told to go and see, and there was the two brothers' address at the top of the list. I reflected that a man who had been unwise enough to say that he had plenty of money probably had an employee capable of training a seven-year-old. I went with him to the farm, without warning or explanation.

When we arrived, we found the horse yoked to a 'Hunter hoe', scuffling turnips. True, one brother drove while the other led the horse, but he seemed quite placid. When my buyer wanted to see the horse ridden, I volunteered, but was quickly put in my place by one of the brothers. 'Don't mind her,' he said, 'She's in dread.' And he swarmed up on the horse's bare back.

They asked for, and got, the same outrageous price they had asked me, but with rather more justification this time. I'd like to be able to say that he was a success, but in England he turned out to be just about impossible. His new owner told me in a letter that the bay had an insensitive mouth and no respect for his rider. '... there's no bucking, no rearing or plunging, just plain, straightforward bloody-mindedness. He's as strong as a bull and as obstinate as a mule ...' A few days later, I met one of the brothers at a farm sale and he asked after the horse.

'He's in Leicestershire,' I said. 'They're finding him hard to manage.'

'Of course they are. He's lonesome – he was our pet. Write to the harmless man and tell him to give the horse five or six mangolds every night and plenty of work in chains. He'll be no trouble at the hunt if he's scuffled half an acre of Swedes first.'

I passed on the advice, but it wasn't acknowledged and I suspect wasn't followed.

*

Buying off the land could be a protracted business; in fairs one had to be speedy. I deliberately didn't use the word 'quick', as this is jargon for dishonest and might be misinterpreted. The horse fairs weren't anything like as rough and lawless as they have been represented, but buying bargains means quick decisions and actions, in fairs as in chain stores. As for violence, much depends on what you mean by it. I went to a big furniture auction and emerged bruised, battered and without any furniture. Normally peaceful citizens, mostly female, weighed in with hands, knees and sometimes feet in their determination to be to the fore. A small-town horse fair was a mild and gentle affair by comparison. A sheep sale, where the buyers crowd round the pens (and I mean crowd), is rougher than any fair I have attended. And if that isn't rough enough for you, try a football match. The point is that, if you are looking for violence, it is, and always has been, easily found.

Some people were well known for their fragile tempers and awkward dispositions, and dealers who didn't want trouble avoided them. I never had any problems with them. There was one character who, although popular and easy-going, had a knack of finding himself in the middle of any rough-house that was going on. He never sought trouble but always found it – the exception that proves the rule. Possibly the company he kept had something to do with it.

This man, whom I will call Joe, had twice been attacked by a bad lot and had come off worst both times. Word went round that the attacker carried a knife, so I will call him Mac. Joe, Mac and their friends all frequented a pub in whose back room many differences had been sorted out. Joe's friends warned him about Mac's knife. They decided things had gone far enough and that it was time Mac cooled his heels in prison for a while.

Accordingly Joe, who was tall and stout, got his friends to wrap him from armpits to knees in a feather quilt, which they tied round him with string. A very large belted mackintosh completed the outfit. Joe planned to taunt Mac into drawing the knife, reckoning that the feathers would turn the blade. He would have all the witnesses he needed.

Joe's friends weren't happy. Some urged him to stay in the shadows because of his overstuffed appearance; all besought him to keep away from the walls. Joe began to wonder if his idea was as good as he'd thought at first.

Mac arrived, spoiling for a fight, but he was bright as well as vicious and took in the situation at a glance. He punched Joe hard on the nose – not a matter for prison – and Joe, hampered by his quilt, crashed on to the floor. Mac then sat on him, drew the knife and used it to rip up the quilt, filling the room with musty feathers. He then left, and nobody tried to stop him.

Most dealers who got involved with the seamy side of horse fairs were poor men. They were born dealers (like me), people who would rather sell at a loss and buy a worse one than not sell at all.

There is something to be said for this point of view. Some horses bought on spec are hard to place, even when they are good ones. Billy Bamlet, who bought so many of mine, used to ask if I had any 'dangling in the branches'. I often sold him a horse for cost or less when I had got tired of looking at it. Anything is better than swapping – the ultimate face-saver. The swapped-with may get rid of his misfits, but the instigator of the swap always comes off worst. When he realizes this, he may swap again, losing every time. In the end, he will, as they say, be left with nothing but the halter.

Swapping in kind is a much better idea. I have always liked what is called a tinker's deal, when, instead of changing a bad horse for a worse one, you exchange him for a good cow or a suitable number of sheep. I have done both these things. I knew a man who once exchanged two cows for a litter of pigs and a piano, but he was drunk at the time. His wife, who had asked him to buy her a piano, was pleased, but thought he might have wrapped it up before loading it in the lorry with the pigs.

John went along with my passion for dealing, although he didn't share it. As long as I kept my hands off our breeding stock he was content to let me sell everything else. He did sometimes object to the people I dealt with, and he was usually right. One man had bought quite a number of horses from us, and I said at intervals, 'He's all right – you're just prejudiced.' He wasn't all right, as we discovered to our cost.

An elderly woman summed him up nicely. 'I wouldn't lie against him for shelter,' she said. 'Not if I had to go to Connacht for a bush.'

CHAPTER TWENTY

Weather and Clocks

Over the years I have had many dealings with European buyers of both horses and dogs. Most of them spoke English at least as good as mine, but I have sometimes had to try to deal in my frightful French. Now if it's hard to make small talk in a language you are bad at it's the very devil to try to make money in it. None of the phrase books tell you how to say, 'The bay gelding you bid me for has pulled his stifle,' or 'I mated the smaller bitch with Casey's good doubles dog, but she didn't hold.'

In the end, I gave up and just translated everything literally, using a dictionary. The results reduced my French, Belgian and Swiss customers to fits of laughter, but they got the gist. My school dictionary was too coy to give a word for in season.

'*Elle est en saison*,' I said.

'*Pardon?*'

'*Elle est sur* – oh God, what's heat? *Elle est chaud. Elle veut s'encoupler.*'

'*Pardon?*'

Dutch people seem to speak excellent English. One of them arrived here wanting to hire a horse for a day's hunting. The exception that proves the rule, he conversed in sign language. Like me, he had a phrase book; like mine, it wasn't helpful. We didn't as a rule hire out horses, but as he couldn't get one elsewhere, offered him a plain little chestnut which had been the 'blender' in a bunch of three. Too small for a trooper, he was quiet if little else. The Dutchman searched his phrase book and summed him up with masterly understatement. 'I think,' he said, 'he will not make history.'

For the next day's hunting, this gentleman acquired a hireling from someone else; a brown animal, known to some of us as Scrubbing Brush. This horse had a rooted objection to jumping. The Dutchman, a good horseman, set him at a low, solid rail. Scrubbing Brush galloped at it, stopped dead, did a vertical takeoff, cracked the rail with his heels and dropped like a brick, landing heavily on all four feet. As his unfortunate rider was flung into the air, then deposited violently on the front of the saddle, he yelled, '*Gerr ... bloot ... boogaire!*'

'You know,' said John to me, 'I believe I could learn Dutch.' I forget if it was this Dutchman or another who said, in careful phrases, 'Ireland is beautiful, but you have no sun and no clocks.' Though I denied this with some force, he did have a point.

Weather is, I suppose, the greatest enemy of the farmer, and in Ireland bad weather means rain. We don't, thank God, get snowed up; we do get bogged down.

There is, of course, a well-worn fallacy about Ireland, namely that it is full of bogs. This is untrue, as is the other fallacy – that the bog idea is nonsense. I live on limestone land which drains overnight. Only five miles away there is a string of bogs reaching away into the midlands.

Bogs don't just sit there; they move about. Their movement is hardly perceptible until a roadway collapses or a building suddenly subsides. I remember asking a farmer if it was safe to cross a certain bog on a horse. He said he thought not. 'Two calves drowned just there,' he said, pointing. 'The roars of them was unmerciful.'

'Here?' I asked, mystified. 'Yes. Just there, where you're standing.' This happened to be on the main Cloughjordan road, some way from the dangerous area. Further questioning established that the calves had met their end some fifty years earlier. The bog had moved about twenty yards in the interval.

This place, Lofty Bog, is one of a chain of three, divided by lanes and roads. 'Lofty' is a popular site for seagulls wishing to nest undisturbed. It is also a burial ground for dead cars and tractors. One day, as I was riding towards a pub called Luckybags, I noticed that a piece of rusty machinery had been dumped at the edge of the bog. It was some sort of antique compressor and was at least six feet square. As I passed, there was a gulping noise and bubbles of marsh gas broke the surface all round the machine, which lurched and settled a few inches. I was visiting friends for the day. When I returned in the evening the bog had swallowed the compressor completely. Nasty.

About fifty yards from the compressor's grave, a small piece of soundish land was used as a site for a dance hall. Funds were restricted and the land was, rightly, cheap. Known as the 'Floating Ballroom', it had a maple floor and a tin roof. When it rained, the noise drowned the band. It had only been used a few times when water began to seep, then to gush through the cracks in the floor; it was soon abandoned.

Part of the bog was traversed by a causeway wide enough for a donkey and cart, and perfectly safe if you took it quietly. Out hunting, we used to gallop along it, feeling the surface shift from side to side and sometimes heave up and down. This was as unnerving for horses as for their riders, and the keenest would slow up, bewildered. Once, a horse and rider ahead of me suddenly tumbled over sideways for no reason that I could see. 'The road went from under me,' said the rider. He was more or less correct.

Those who imagine that Ireland is just one great swamp often seem to think that bogs are a feature of no other country. I thought so myself until I met a Yorkshire horse dealer (admittedly he was drunk), who argued at great length about the superiority of Yorkshire bogs over the Tipperary variety. He said they were bigger, deeper and wetter, and seemed proud of the fact. 'And the rain is wetter in Ireland,' he said.

'Rubbish. How could it be?'

'It's a well known fact. The drops are closer together.'

*

Bogs are now things to be explored, written about and protected. They have acquired a certain cachet. I got side-tracked on to bogs, when it was my intention to write about mud. There is nothing good to be said about mud, and nothing to beat the misery of it. Rain, sleet and snow cease to fall eventually. Mud is still around when the rain has stopped. In a farmyard after snow, one encounters the worst kind of all: mud evenly mixed with slush and manure.

One of the things which makes me prefer sheep to cows is that they are so much cleaner. The farmyard used to be dominated by a vast manure heap. Who ever heard of a constipated cow? Nowadays there are slurry tanks which are at least underground, but it's a good idea to shut the windows when they are being emptied.

In the early days of one of the farming organizations, some sensitive souls decided that the word 'dung' should be banned. Instead, farmers were asked to call this substance FYM, farmyard manure, pronounced 'fim'. I never heard anyone do this. People not born to farming often develop an uncanny interest in its nastier aspects, which seems strange to one who is crafty at avoiding them. One 'new-catched' farmer, as John used to call them, cordially invited us to go with him to a slurry-handling demonstration and was quite put out when we refused.

Thinking back to the years when I never missed a horse fair, I am almost glad those days have gone. If you have orders for horses, then horses you must buy, come hell or high water. Today you can buy in cushioned comfort at Kill, if that's your line, and all sales are under cover. There was no comfort at the fairs, which took place regardless of the weather.

Three years in a row Cahirmee fair in July was almost washed out. I know; I bought twelve horses at those three watery events and spent around ten hours in wet clothes at each. I galloped horses for their wind in paddocks where they sank almost to their knees. In fact, it was possible to trot them for their wind – a couple of rounds had them blowing hard enough for any weakness to be obvious.

At one of these fairs I was caught in a thunderstorm which left me so drenched I couldn't possibly go to a café for a meal. There didn't seem to be a shop which stocked anything for women, except cardigans and corsets, neither of which was priority just then. I found one, specializing in menswear, with a notice up: CLOSING DOWN SALE. EVERYTHING MUST GO. There I bought a shirt and a pair of jeans.

As I needed to put them on, I asked if there was a changing-room. The assistant looked doubtful, but showed me upstairs and indicated a dark, cluttered room, where I could see little besides a bed and some stacks of cardboard boxes. There was a bath-towel hanging over a chair, so I undressed and towelled myself dry. Then I put on the new clothes and sat on the side of the bed to lace my shoes. A polite voice beside me said, 'Good evening, miss.' There was an old man in the bed. Since then, I have examined all changing-rooms carefully.

The rain flooded the whole town, and the only people who weren't cursing it were the evangelical preachers, a feature of this fair and of Kilrush, who continued to preach with commendable enthusiasm, although they had no audience.

On cold days, buyers on their way home from Kilrush fair congregated at Fanny O'Dea's at Lissycasey to be restored by Fanny's famous egg-flips, laced with brandy. I generally pretended to be teetotal when dealing – it was easy then to keep out of pubs. Pubs on fair days were places to be avoided, but I made an exception of Fanny O'Dea's.

*

I suppose we've grown soft. Nothing the weather could do would deter my parents from driving five miles to church or the shops in the gig. Flood water almost to the shafts was a yearly hazard until our by-road was raised by six feet. Cyclists used to go round by the fields.

I remember one truly appalling day with floods of rain and a Force 10 gale, when my parents were obliged to attend a funeral six miles away. I was taken along to hold the pony while the adults were at the graveside. There was no waterproof footgear other than gumboots to be had, and I can still see my mother standing on one leg emptying the water out of her shoes – with little complaint. Living through this period makes me feel for the coachmen of olden days, perched up on their box-seats in all weathers. No wonder so many of them took to the bottle.

Now that I seldom need to sit for hours in wet clothes or suffer the pain of chilblains, I sometimes wonder if there is much to be said for the Spartan life. Does it benefit anybody? And if so, why is it so bad for animals? Cold is less of an enemy than rain and wind. Shelter is the first requisite for animals in the winter. If they feel cold they eat more to keep their energy up, and are subject to infections and lung disorders. This applies to cattle, sheep and horses, so why not to grooms and shepherds too? Stuffy stables and low, crowded buildings are almost as bad but not quite. I have never known animals which had shelter and space to breathe come to much harm.

Sheep in particular are good weather prophets. They hate the wet and start moving to a sheltered part of the field well before the rain arrives. They lie down when it's going to rain as cattle do. Having eaten well while the grass was dry, they lie down to digest the meal. Then they move to the driest place they can find.

Of course our foxhunting Dutchman, like many others, only encountered Irish weather in the depths of winter, so his opinions were biased. But what of his other statement, that we have no clocks? We have; we just don't consult them very often.

I was trained in punctuality from an early age by my ex-army father, and such habits stick. I still keep time myself, but don't expect my countrymen to do likewise. It's a mistake to think that Irish people get pleasure from being late; we are, as a race, indifferent to the passage of time. This must surely reduce the incidence of stress-related diseases.

One true story neatly sums up what I am trying to say. An Englishman, a lorry-driver, had moved to Ireland and was looking for a job. He applied to the owner of a haulage business, and made an appointment to meet him at his home at 8 a.m. the following morning.

At 8 o'clock sharp, Bill was ringing the haulier's doorbell. Then he decided the bell wasn't working and thumped the knocker. After a time, a window above his head opened, and a lady in her night-dress looked out. 'What the hell do you want?'

'I want to see the boss. I have an appointment for 8 o'clock.'

The haulier's wife consulted her watch. 'Why, it's only 8 o'clock now,' she exclaimed, and left Bill, a sadder and wiser man, to wait in his car until a more Christian hour.

CHAPTER TWENTY-ONE

Sheep on the Cheap

When John and I were married, the recession in farming was coming to an end. Everybody was being encouraged to take out huge loans and 'think big'. What a contrast to the running battle I had carried on with the bank for so many years! The immediate result was that some farmers did indeed think big and, with the help of massive cash injections, progressed from being small farmers to being large, even enormous farmers. Many thought too big, and went out of business.

Naturally, our horse-dealing business depended on loans, but only those we knew we could meet. Neither of us had ever been in a position to avail of the aid being offered, and so we did without. Luckily for us, as a sudden leap in interest rates did for a lot of people.

Being confined to the house more than I was used to, as I couldn't expect John to take to the perpetual picnic which my life had been for years, I wanted a small enterprise to carry out on my own. I bought thirty in-lamb ewes. Thinking small, you see. Now, the popular idea of a small farmer has changed surprisingly little with the passing of time. He may be shown as a carefree character, strolling about among his livestock and presumably living on fresh air. The other popular image is of an embittered slave, trudging through the slurry in leaky boots, working eighteen hours a day, seven days a week, in order to survive. Equally untrue.

My sheep were a viable enterprise as long as they were housed. As soon as they went out to grass I had problems. John had a good dog by then, and offered to lend him, but the ewes were my thing – I refused. Even a modest farming operation is viable if carried out by one person. As soon as you reach a point where you have to pay for help, there is such a huge jump in expenditure that you have to buy more stock. Which means borrowing.

'If you won't work Roy, you'd better have a dog of your own,' said John. He pointed out that a dog is on call day or night, all the year round, doesn't appreciate a holiday, but is eager to get back to its work and will go until it drops. This is not normally the outlook of a human helper – indeed it shouldn't be. There is no need to live a dog's life unless you are a dog.

I said firmly that I could manage. I couldn't, of course. The sheep were a wild bunch, and I couldn't get near enough to them to count them. I couldn't round them up – the field was large. I did my herding from the back of a horse, as today some use motorbikes. The snag about either horse or bike is that while you are opening a gate for the flock, they will have quickly hurried back to where they came from. While you are shutting the gate, having fetched them again, they may go anywhere. One thing they won't do is wait quietly in a bunch.

'I'll teach them to follow a tin of nuts,' I said. They didn't need teaching. I was sometimes in danger of being trampled under foot with my tin of nuts. Wherever I went, there was an eager, bleating, barging crowd at my heels; I couldn't get away from the brutes.

The reason why I was so reluctant to use a dog was that John was an outstanding sheepdog handler, and I felt intimidated by his professional approach. I was afraid of spoiling the dog and of making a fool of myself. I read books on sheep management instead. One of these books gave a list of necessities for a lambing flock, a list too long and too boring to quote. John said three of the most important items were missing – plenty of Massey-Harris band, twice as many spare light bulbs as you think you will need, and a good dog.

Massey-Harris band is Yorkshire for baling twine, and of course John was right. The first time I had to deliver a lamb unassisted (at an hour unpopular with vets and neighbours alike), the ewe refused to lie still. I doubled a length of twine, tied it round a front fetlock with a plough knot, drew the leg upward, passed the twine across the back of the ewe's neck, pulled it tight and attached the end to the other foreleg. Like it or not, and I suspect that she didn't, the ewe had to lie still. A piece of soft rope would have been better but none was to hand and the twine worked. Calves used to be trussed up like this when in transit in car boots.

Baling twine takes the place of wire, of rope, of staples and, occasionally, of braces. People say it's the badge of the lazy farmer. This to me is like insisting on tying sheaves while the combine stands idle. I was short of time and help. I improvised whenever possible. To this day, I use baling twine for every conceivable purpose. Most of the gates on the farm have wire mesh fastened along their bottoms to discourage young lambs from creeping underneath. Yes, you may laugh at the little knots of blue and yellow twine which have replaced the wire fasteners, but the twine will last and can be tied on in minutes, so why not? I think they look rather pretty. For some jobs, twine isn't strong enough, even doubled, but six thicknesses plaited make an almost unbreakable cord. These cords make blue and yellow leads for dogs, halters for horses and fasteners for gates.

My ewes were lucky. Still refusing the help of a dog, I kept them in a shed right under the windows when lambing time came round. I was expecting to have to rush out every couple of hours to make sure that all was well, but John reassured me. He told me to leave them alone from midnight until 6 a.m., unless one had started to lamb. He said I'd soon be an inefficient wreck if I didn't get enough sleep, and that the ewes wouldn't benefit from constantly being woken up any more than I would. He taught me to fill the hay racks after the midnight inspection, reckoning the ewes would lamb when they had fed and rested. Feeding at 6, he said, was simply asking for a rush of lambs at 3 a.m.

For thirty years, I followed his advice and hardly ever regretted it. City-dwellers, who think of lambing time as one long stint in the maternity ward, may doubt this. Actually, the after-care and feeding of the ewes and their lambs takes up more time. Herding is the very essence of 'dog-and-stick' farming. I watched John, and wondered how to back down gracefully on the subject of a dog. Without one, you must walk right round the field, counting heads. Ewes leave their young lambs hidden when they go to feed, and finding them is time consuming. As soon as a dog appears in the field, even the familiar one they see every day, every ewe will call her lambs to her, so checking them takes only a few minutes.

Of course my thirty ewes were only a fraction of our sheep enterprise. John and the dogs were managing another 275 with much less fuss. Quite a number of new sheep farmers used to ask his advice, and I remember an earnest young man asking, 'What shall I do about my lambing average?'

'Do the same as everyone else,' said John cynically. 'Lie about it.'

*

The sheep tied in pretty well with our horse-dealing. We didn't have much trade in the winter months, and there were no big fairs until Kilrush on March 25th. This was a day when John was content to sheep-sit, and I went to the fair on my own. Usually though, we went everywhere together. If one of us appeared alone, fellow dealers would ask, 'Where's the other one?'

I looked after the sheep when John was out hunting, and it was on one of these occasions that he fell and broke his leg, leaving me in charge of 350 ewes which had just started lambing.

This experience was unpleasant for John, who was sadly neglected. It did me a great deal of good, as it taught me just how much I could do. It also forced me to use that dog.

*

The dog in question was called Roy. Later, he served as a model for another Roy, a dog in a novel called *No Harp Like My Own*. Roy had had a hard life and was touchy and suspicious. Few could win his confidence, let alone his affection. John succeeded, and so did I to a lesser extent. We were careful to keep him away from Diana, then a baby, but Roy was different with her; patient and affectionate.

Once I had got used to working the sheep with Roy, I became bitten (to coin a phrase) with sheepdogs and sheepdog trials. John gave me a Border Collie bitch for myself, and I was soon breeding and selling puppies. The Crannagh kennel was registered around 1970.

*

Our horse business was narrowing. In the early seventies, as farming boomed, the demand for horses fell away. The police trade dwindled as the 'Troubles' in Northern Ireland worsened, and the Swiss Army took to motorbikes. We still had customers for riding horses, but the horse boats were being replaced by containers. In these, one had to send a load of six in order for it to pay, and it no longer paid to send anything except high-class animals. We had been used to mixing in a two-year-old or two and perhaps a cob, as the cost of six broken three-year-olds was beyond us most of the time. Even then, the rocketing cost of transport was way ahead of the rise in price of horses. We began to consider breeding one or two.

Compared with dealing, breeding is a dead loss. The saying 'fools breed horses for wise men to buy' is, I think, true of half-breds. The land occupied by our three mares, if ploughed out, would have shown a much higher return. Keeping horses is a disease, like betting on them. We always sold foals, as they certainly didn't pay to keep any longer. I continued to keep a couple of mares for several years after I was widowed. We bred some good horses, but often the breeder was the last person to hear what had happened to his foal. This is not the case today, and one gets credit – if no cash – for breeding something special. My best (as far as I know) was the show jumper Abervail Dream, which I sold to Dr Noel Cawley for about £1000. His value today would be hard to estimate.

My first incursion into horse-breeding was an unwilling one. My mare, Matilda, an extraordinary performer and a great character, seemed to be indestructible. She jumped blind ditches, galloped down rock-strewn hillsides, pushed her way through thorn hedges, never getting a mark. Then one day, jumping a low bushed-up gap she'd popped over a hundred times, she picked up a blackthorn. She got blood poisoning, then lymphangitis and was never sound again.

I sent Matilda to a local stallion, a young horse. She wasn't in foal, so I was promised a free return. The next year, I wrote to the stallion owner, saying I'd send her back. He replied, '... there may not be many more foals by my horse, as the poor lad is, alas, made a gelding of ...'. I like the word 'many'.

It was three years before Matilda obliged with a foal. Then she had three fillies in three years, then nothing. After a further five years of fruitless trips to various stallions and expensive treatment, I gave up, and Matilda lived in idleness until she died at the age of twenty-eight. The three fillies were all very good indeed. They show-jumped, evented and were wonderful hunters. But none reached 16 hands, none paid for her keep. The old saying was true. I joined the wise men and bought horses bred by others.

When I was vetting my own horses in the fairs, I learned not only to look out for soundness but to ask about stable vices (such as crib-biting or weaving). I also asked, in the case of mares, 'Could she be in foal?'

A friend of mine once bought a pony filly for £5 when I was just starting to deal. She was only 11 hands and was to be a first pony for my friend's little girl. About a week later, in October, she produced a foal. Where she'd been carrying it was anybody's guess, as she'd shown no signs of pregnancy beforehand. The foal was yellow in colour, with a tightly curled woolly coat and blue eyes. It was about as big as a large dog. I believe it eventually reached 14.2 hands and was referred to as a Palomino. I never saw it after the ugly-duckling stage and, let's face it, they usually grow into ugly ducks rather than swans.

I remembered that foal whenever I was bidding for a mare and asked hastily, 'Could she be in foal?' The thought of a Metropolitan Police horse producing a yellow foal with blue eyes was too horrible to contemplate. The question was seldom well received. Reactions varied from a snapped 'Of course not', through blank astonishment to outraged denial. Yet, I managed to buy at least half a dozen mares which were in foal and weren't supposed to be.

After I hurt my back, I looked round for a real 'armchair' to take me hunting. I was back on a horse almost as soon as I was out of plaster but, although he was quiet, I simply couldn't bear his trot. I taught him to break into a canter from a walk and discovered that I couldn't bear his canter either, so I went to Kilrush fair. At Kilrush, I bought three brown horses, one very large and two quite small, otherwise almost identical. (My mother named them collectively, 'The Chesterfield Suite'.) The large horse, or sofa as it were, was a mare with the easiest paces I'd ever known. I sold the two smaller and younger elements of the suite and kept the mare, which I called Rosalind.

When after a time I got bored with Rosalind and felt I could cope with something livelier, I passed her on to a lady in Sussex. It crossed my mind that all was not well with the mare, that she shouldn't be so lazy, so I got a vet to examine her heart and she passed. Two months later, the owner's son jumped a clear round with her at the local riding stable. 'She'll do even better when you've got all that meat off her,' said the proprietor. Suddenly, Rosalind pawed the ground and lay down. 'Colic! Fetch the vet!'

By the time the vet arrived, Rosalind had produced a bay filly of unknown pedigree. Named Amazing Grace, she was winning jumping events at four years old. It was an occasion when I expected abuse and got thanks instead.

A few weeks later, I spent ages looking for a mare for a special order. My instructions were so precise, involving colour and markings to match another horse, that I thought I'd have to give up. Then I found exactly what I was looking for, as far as I could see, in a sale. The mare was by No Complaint, and the new owner proposed to name her after her sire.

I bought three horses in the sale, and could fit only two into my trailer, so I paid for overnight stabling for No Complaint II. When I returned the next day, I found that thieves had relieved her of her headcollar, all four shoes and most of her tail. The loss of the headcollar and shoes was a nuisance, that of her tail a disaster. I rang up the owner, expecting the deal to be off, but he told me to send her on. I had bought the mare complete with vet's certificate, but she turned out to be in foal.

I then contacted the man I'd bought her from, who said, 'I swear on my honour that the mare is a virgin.' His neighbours told me on the quiet that tinkers had been camped nearby and they had a jackass with them. The mare might well produce a mule. Instead, she gave birth to quite a reasonable sort of filly of Irish draught type. I was relieved to hear that its ears were of normal length. Somewhere along the line, No Complaint II's name was changed.

I was right to be worried, though. Years later, a brood mare was sold in Ballinasloe for cash. The seller, a stranger to the locality, said she was in foal to Old Jack. Questioned about Old Jack, he said he was a purebred stallion but not in the book. In due course, the mare produced a mule, and all attempts to trace her former owner failed.

*

While on the subject of foals, legitimate and otherwise, I can't resist telling the story of a certain man whose work necessitated the use of a horse and cart. These were provided by the man's employer, whose knowledge of horses was nil. The horse in question was a mare.

It occurred to the man, as he drove the cart to and fro every day, that the mare's potential was sadly wasted. She was leading an unfulfilled life, his wages were barely adequate. If she were to produce a foal in her spare time, it would augment his wages and harm nobody.

Around mid-April, he found it necessary to ask if he might have the shafts of the cart widened. He rejected the idea of giving the mare less to eat. Anybody, he said, who knew anything about horses, was aware of the unique fattening qualities of hay in mid-April. His employer had not been aware of any such thing, but rather than admit his ignorance, he paid for alterations to the cart.

Shortly afterwards, the mare contracted a mysterious illness and had to be rested. The man who worked her said he would take her to his own home where she would be cared for properly. This he did, and, after a time, the mare was able to resume her normal work. She had lost a great deal of weight and the shafts had to be altered again.

The story eventually got round to the man's employer, but he felt too foolish to make a fuss about it.

CHAPTER TWENTY-TWO

The Horse on the Half Crown

I have always liked buying horses in County Clare, just a few miles west as the crow flies, but divided from my county, Tipperary, by the waters of Lough Derg. It was in West Clare that John and I bought Roll-On.

When Ireland produced a 20p coin, I was delighted to renew acquaintance with an old friend – the horse on the half crown. The pre-decimal coinage was most attractive, and many people would like to see the pig, the hen, the hare and the greyhound revived, along with the bull, the salmon and, of course, the horse.

One June day John and I went to Spancilhill fair in search of Swiss troopers. We bought a couple but, as usual at this fair, they were neither very good nor very cheap. We were about to give up and go in search of food when we were approached by an enormously tall, stooping, elderly man. 'Are you the man and the woman?' he asked. 'Wait now, I'll think of the name in a minute.'

'Quarton,' said John.

'That's it. I have a way of remembering it. I say, "He's not a pint 'un, he's a quart 'un," but I had it forgotten. Do you want to buy a good trooper? If you come to my place, I have him. The perfect trooper.'

'What's he like?'

'He's like the horse on the half crown.'

We studied a half crown and agreed that it might be worth seeing. The perfect trooper was a compact animal with quality, 15.2 to 16 hands high, with good carriage and straight action. Troopers had to use their hocks well, with no hint of dragging toes.

The Swiss had an unusual way of allocating their troopers, which meant that they needed a constant supply. On arrival, they were screened, and anything with showjumping potential was taken out for training. Each of the remainder, after breaking and schooling, was allocated to a young man starting his compulsory National Service. When the man's spell of duty was completed, he was given his horse at a subsidized price to take home to the family farm. This was the reason for insistence on good action, back and front, and the preference for active, hardy types. Greys were not used, although the Swiss Mounted Police rode greys.

As there was a fairly low price limit and the usual factor of two or three middlemen all claiming a share, more mares than geldings went abroad; and of the bigger, better quality animals, most were mares. A good gelding would cost up to half as much again as a mare. These mares were a loss to breeders, but in the sixties, the armies and the police were the best customers for them.

The horse on the half crown sounded just the thing for Dick Morgan, the shipping agent who bought most of our troopers. The tall man, whom I will call Denis, went ahead to his farm twenty miles away, to smarten his horse up, he said, while we paused for a meal in Ennis.

The directions Denis had given us were good, and we had no difficulty in finding his farm. There was a white gate leading onto a lane, with a high thorn hedge on either side of it. On the left, a row of sturdy ash saplings grew in the hedge. I was driving, and as I drove up the lane, a rope seemed suddenly to rise up from the ground ahead and stretch itself out in our path at a height of about three feet.

We thought we were seeing things and I managed to stop just in time. John got out of the car and found that one end of the rope was tied to an ash tree. The other end disappeared through the opposite hedge, and was attached to the headcollar of a chestnut horse. The rope was about thirty feet long, and the horse had tightened it by moving away when he heard the car.

As he stood there, with his head high, chestnut all over, the end of his tail squared off level with his hocks, he was indeed the image of the horse on the half crown. There was something unusual about his appearance: in addition to a headcollar with a white browband and brass buckles, he wore, by way of a roller, a red inner tube out of a bicycle tyre.

While we were examining this, Denis appeared on the scene. John remarked that we might have run into the rope, but he dismissed this. He explained that there was nothing strong enough to tie a horse to in the other hedge. 'I knew, being strangers, you'd be driving handy,' he said. The chestnut moved as well as he looked. By an Irish draught called Golden Plover, he must have had good breeding on his dam's side as he had no feather and lovely light action. He was, as Denis had said, the perfect trooper.

One thing puzzled us – the bicycle tube. It hadn't been cut, there was air in it. How had Denis got it on?

'Ah, it was easy,' said Denis. He pulled the tube back along the horse's body, over his hindquarters, and let it drop to the ground. Then he bent down, standing directly behind the chestnut, with his face a few inches from its heels, and lifted the tube up, over and into place again. 'It makes him look smart, doesn't it?' he said.

'Did you break him in yourself?' I asked.

'He isn't trained at all. He never had a bit in his mouth in his life.'

We bought the horse for a good price, for he was special, and arranged to collect him another day. We decided to name him Roll-On after the elastic girdles worn by overweight women at the time.

When we returned with a trailer, Roll-On was tethered, not to the ash tree, but to a pair of heavy, iron-shod wheels on an axle. This ingenious, if rather risky, arrangement meant that the horse could graze where he liked, hauling the wheels after him, but he couldn't get through a gap and was easily caught.

In due course, Dick Morgan bought Roll-On and he went to Switzerland. A charming natured horse – we were sorry to part with him. Later, we bought his half sister, but she was different in every way, and must have given some unfortunate Swiss recruit a lively time. Owing to her habit of lying down when annoyed, we called her Swiss Roll.

*

Roll-On was reared near Miltown Malbay. I've never forgotten arriving at this small seaside town early on a frosty morning for the fair. I don't believe that any tropical ocean could be bluer than the Atlantic was that day, and frost edged the lanes with white lace.

The fair was no good, and I didn't go to it again, but I did return to the west coast on frosty winter days as well as sunny summer ones, for that is when it is most beautiful; then and on a June morning around 6 a.m. Next to Cahirmee, the Kilrush June fair became my favourite. I would stay in Kilkee, and there was keen pleasure in driving into the fair on a fine June morning.

The first time I went to Kilrush, when I was struggling, my funds didn't run to a night in a B&B and I drove down in the morning. This was the October fair, and I left home at 6 a.m. in a thick fog. A car and trailer had gone off the road at the old hump-backed bridge at Bunratty, and another was in the ditch farther on. I arrived at the fair feeling as tired as if I'd done a day's work.

Although I hadn't been to Kilrush fair before, I'd been on a buying trip in the area. I'd had a letter from a Kilrush man I'd bought from in Limerick fair. It was addressed to 'The Horse Woman called Margarine who lives near Nenagh.' To the credit of the Post Office, it arrived with little delay.

Dear Margarine,
I am the man with the horse you got. I have 2 more. Come before the fair, as it is full of hooks and eyes. Cheerio for now ...

I would defy anyone to ignore a letter like that. Disappointingly, the two horses were very ordinary, so I left them to the hooks and eyes and looked elsewhere. Not knowing anybody – or, just as important, being known – makes it difficult to find the right farms. I'd already wasted a day in another county being taken about by two gentlemen who were interested only in relieving their friends of useless animals. They talked all the time, both at once. Afterwards, I discovered that they were known in their locality as Bullshit and Blethering Mick. I did buy one horse off the land, but the time involved made it uneconomic; after that, I went to the fairs when I could.

Every time I went to Kilrush, there seemed to be more chestnuts about. Owing to the English prejudice against them, especially chestnut mares, dealers tended to avoid them. Kilrush was fairly crawling with them. Having owned Marigold and Echo, I might have been expected to give them a wide berth myself, but I'd come to the conclusion that only certain types of chestnut were bad to do with. I think it's more to do with the skin than the colour. Chestnut colour, especially the all-over, rather metallic variety, combined with a thin skin, meant trouble more often than not. But there is a type of carrot-coloured chestnut with a skin like a carpet, which is more often a slug. Ultra-thin skin is often found on all-over browns and dark greys, but not on bays or bay-browns. More trouble. Marigold and Echo were both thin-skinned. One of my best-ever police horses was a chestnut mare, but she had a skin like a Hereford bullock and was about as emotional as a dinner table.

By the end of the fifties, it wasn't unusual to see a group of six or eight horses heading for Kilrush, every one a chestnut. 'Where are all the chestnuts coming from?' I asked a local man.

'They're Rosebuds.' he replied.

'They're what?'

'They're by a stallion called Rosebud,' he amplified his statement. Whoever heard of a stallion called Rosebud? He was chestnut (naturally), by Ypres Rose. His progeny were known for their jumping ability and their placid natures. They were often big and flashy with white markings, and the geldings were snapped up for police work.

Because of their serene temperaments, many Rosebuds were saddled for the first time just before the fair. One, a great big showy fellow, looked to be just what I needed for a great big fat man, whose nerve wasn't the best. I asked if I might ride the horse and the owner gave me a leg up. The horse set off at a gentle trot down the street, ears pricked. He would neither stop nor turn and hadn't the ghost of a mouth. As he was all of 17 hands, I didn't fancy jumping off, so we trotted gently on, past the hotel, past some warehouses, until I began to wonder if he was going to trot gently into the Shannon estuary. I turned him by hitting the side of his face with the end of the reins, and we trotted gently back.

'How often has this brute been ridden?' I demanded angrily, when I was safely on the ground.

'Twice. Yesterday and today.'

The big fat man didn't get this horse, but I bought him and, after a spell in breaking tackle, he turned out well.

Rosebud sired some good jumpers; two which I bought in Kilrush were Tannoch Brae and Bud. Bud was bought for a trooper, but Dick Morgan left him because he was rather narrow. So we decided to hunt him for the season, and offer him again when age might have broadened him. John and I decided to clip him out and we did all one side of him, including his head. Bud, true to his breed, made no objection. Then it happened. As John was reaching up to clip Bud's ear, they both got an electric shock. Bud leaped in the air, banging his head on a beam and bringing down a shower of plaster and cobwebs. He spun round, lashed out and fled. John and I, caught with a right and left, were sent crashing into different corners of the stable. We both got cuts on our heads, necessitating stitches and anti-tets. John also got a hefty shock from the faulty cable.

We picked ourselves up and limped off, cursing, to look for Bud. We found him down by the river, trotting about in that disjointed way horses do when they know they've no business to be loose. He was a true Rosebud, however, and allowed himself to be caught and led home. Before we had recovered from our injuries, Michael Moran from Askeaton had bought him, and he later made a Guinness Championship finalist at four years old and was exported to Switzerland. Michael hunted him for the rest of the season, but he never succeeded in clipping the other side of him.

I used to spend the evening before Kilrush fair looking at some of the horses which were to be sold next day. I'd go to the blacksmith's shop, where the unbroken colts waited, queued up for a pair of front shoes apiece. The old smith did the job faster than one would have thought possible. No matter how violently the horse objected, he would hoist up a foreleg and, mouth full of nails, hammer on a shoe like lightening. Every so often, he would pause long enough to drain a pint of stout at a single draught. The ready-made shoes came in three sizes, had no clip and were about three-quarters of an inch thick. The colts, unaccustomed to the weight, would have been easier to sell unshod with their feet dressed. As it was, they picked them up like hackneys and were disinclined to step out for fear of slipping.

I bought some good jumpers in Kilrush besides the two I mentioned. Spanish John was an international horse, Strauss and The Graduate were two useful winners. John's favourite hunter, Harvey, came from Kilrush too.

*

Fairs were much better for dealers than auction sales. In theory, if there aren't enough good horses to go round in a sale, the person with the most money will get them all. Reality is different, with buyers forming 'rings' and 'standing out' for each other. The chances of getting a good bargain by quick-wittedness or seeing it first are gone.

The first horse auction I attended was in Gort, Co. Galway, around 1966 – and was fiercely opposed by dealers. I'd no intention of going until an anonymous caller rang up and ordered me to stay away. I have never taken kindly to being told where I may or may not go, especially by someone who won't give his name. So I went (only one other dealer did) and bought two troopers. If the horses on offer had been better, we'd have had a field day, but they were moderate.

Those who have always dealt privately or at auction often fail to see the need for a third person to make a price. There is no need when friends or business associates are involved. A figure can be agreed on – or not. No amount of shouting and hand-slapping would make any difference.

I have mentioned 'tanglers' or 'guinea-hunters'. They not only line their own pockets but save face for both parties. If A swears by all that is holy that he won't sell for less than a thousand and B says he'd rather die than give more than eight hundred, it is hard for either to be the first to climb down. Enter C, who puts his arms round the shoulders of A and B and suggests they meet at nine hundred, which is exactly what both want to do anyway. Grudgingly, A and B agree to split the difference – but only to please C and so as not to break his word. Both claim to be acting against their better judgment, no face is lost and C collects from one or both parties.

Any lamb, pigeon or mush who may be reading this should be warned. There is no compulsion to give any outsider anything unless you have asked for his help. When I first bought in fairs, every deal I made attracted a large and noisy crowd. Afterwards, up to a dozen men unknown to me would ask for 'a couple of quid for making the deal for you'. I had no money to give them, so no dangerous precedent was established. I paid about three men I knew from different areas – when I felt they had earned it – not otherwise. After a year or so, I had no more trouble.

CHAPTER TWENTY-THREE

Sitting It Out

The farming boom in the early seventies was, of course, a result of joining the Common Market. Like most rocketing rises, it was matched by a crash which put a lot of farmers out of business. We were lucky in having a diversity of projects. The cattle lost out while the horses and sheep saved us. There is nothing like a slump to teach caution – it concentrates the mind wonderfully. I was among the minority who had lived through the Economic War. Younger farmers seemed to think that the EEC would bring permanent riches for a minimum of effort and responded to the current advice to specialize. Too many eggs in one basket often meant the collapse of the whole basketful.

As we sat it out, we increased the lambing flock, as wool was dear and so were the lighweight lambs needed by the new European market. We did without paid labour and took no risks. While the horse business was affected by the recession, our turnover was so fast that we were often buying and selling on the same day – the only way to deal on a falling market.

As for the sheep, when you manage a flock with no help except that of a dog, and with limited means, you have to aim for a high standard of quality in the lambs. When trade is bad, you can still sell good stock, at a bad price. You can go to market and stay there all day with no one, as they say, to ask you where you are going, if your stock is substandard. I was often reminded of the maxims I had learned from my Yorkshire buyers: 'You can run to buy, but they make you stand to sell.' 'Any daft sod can stand on a street corner and buy dear horses – the day you buy is the day you sell.' Both these sayings are applicable to the daft sods who run to buy dear sheep too.

I thought it would be a great idea to try giving the ewes fertility drugs, resulting in litters rather than pairs of lambs, all born within a few days. John pointed out that we would need expensive help and housing to avoid heavy losses and, while science has given us litters of four and five lambs, it has not given us a ewe with more than two teats. Another farmer friend who wasn't impressed by my plan, said, 'I don't think anything of that old bathroom job – the sponging and flushing – it's against the will of God.' There is also the question of luck – like having all your ewes timed to lamb on the worst day in living memory.

Sitting it out when sheep prices collapse isn't as traumatic as trying to feed a herd of cattle that nobody wants to buy. I have had to do both and survived – just. By the time sheep prices slumped, I was a widow. I thought seriously about selling the lot for what they'd fetch and letting the farm. I thought again, and sold the older ewes, keeping all my ewe lambs for breeding instead. This paid in the long run. I began to look round for other ways of staying solvent, among them writing. I bred more sheepdog pups. When obliged to sell the last of my male lambs for half nothing, I instantly replaced them with females, also for half nothing. I am still sitting it out; prices have risen and fallen again. As I write, they are making less than they did twenty years ago, while the cost of living has risen steadily. I am reducing their numbers, but of course I can't resist a deal if I get the chance. Nowadays I deal in antiques, too, and love it. I shall probably strike a good bargain with the undertaker on my deathbed.

*

You might wonder why a farmer needs a dealer to buy sheep from somebody else and sell to him at a profit.

I once asked a newly fledged farmer whether he bought his sheep direct from the mart or from a dealer. He gave me a shocked look and said he did his marketing through an entrepreneur. In other words, he bought from a dealer. There is a whole new language designed to make simple things complicated. The difference between a dealer and an entrepreneur when marketing livestock is roughly the same as the difference between a commercial traveller and a sales representative.

Livestock owners are divided into groups – those who buy and sell their own animals, and those who employ a dealer or commission agent. Others deal with suppliers who are linked with the factories where the animals end up. The last method is popular, being reasonably foolproof. It also acts as a buffer between the cold reality of the factory and the tender-hearted. To my mind, it turns the farmer himself into a middleman, unpaid at that, but he doesn't seem to see it that way.

I have a rooted objection to allowing other people to spend my hard-earned money for me, and often wonder at the number of highly trained young farmers who allow their employees to choose and buy their stock. If the workman is such a good judge, why isn't he farming? The only reason I have been given is that an eye for stock is something you are born with or without, like an ear for music. I don't believe this. If it were true, a stock farmer without that 'eye' would be like a tone-deaf person trying to keep a job in an orchestra. Ability to judge stock can be developed, and I advise would-be buyers to go to the markets and watch the people who buy and sell for a living. They would soon run out of money if they made mistakes.

Having been obliged to buy my own from the start, I made mistakes, but hadn't the cash to make expensive ones. Most of my buying experience has been gained with horses, when one major blunder could spell financial disaster. This has made me careful in buying all stock – no bad thing, I think. A dealer told me years ago to ask myself three questions when buying a horse: Do I like the look of him? Is there improvement in him? Have I a market for him? 'If the answer to all three questions is "yes",' he said, 'You needn't ask yourself whether you can afford to pay for him; you can.' This advice holds good for any kind of livestock and I've followed it ever since.

It's hard, when you are starting out, to screen the advice you are sure to get. 'Wise men don't need it: fools won't take it.' Some has to be followed, all is well meant. It took me a while to resist advice to buy stock that I instinctively disliked. Instinct is often right, and the person who is paying is also going to have to look at the animals, so why not make it as pleasant as possible? The older I get, the more convinced I become that to do something well, you must enjoy it.

*

After the slump comes the recovery. A rising market is, of course, what every dealer needs. In Ireland the price of milk and the price of beef ruled everything else. When they rose, so in due course would the price of mutton, wool, and even riding horses. The first rise in prices that concerned me occurred when I was new to buying horses.

Everywhere there were rumours. 'The police are upping their prices ... so are the Life Guards/Swiss Cavalry/Gunners ...' Even the animals known as 'blood-testers', which were used by veterinary firms for developing vaccines, suddenly rose in price. Ballinasloe fair was full of rumours.

Some of these were started deliberately for a joke. Unlike the street fairs, Ballinasloe attracted as many private buyers as dealers. On the rest of the circuit, you saw the same faces again and again. Ballinasloe was full of strangers. 'That's the Duke of Beaufort. He's looking for hunters, he's loaded.' I don't know how the story started, but the man in question, an Englishman on holiday, was almost mobbed. He looked about him in some alarm as he was surrounded on all sides by people riding or dragging horses which they hoped he would buy. Some blockers tugged at his arms, others shouted or whispered in his ears, according to their preferred technique. Freeing himself with difficulty, he dashed away, probably for a stiff drink in Hayden's Hotel. He didn't reappear.

Many will remember the day of the Russian Buyer. I was there myself at the outset, but didn't suspect where an innocent remark would lead. I was talking to a Galway man named Joe McNamara. We were looking at a bunch of ponies, which had all been sold together to one man. The man was checking their legs and teeth, putting halters on them and so on. Then he pulled out his wallet and counted out a large sum of money in notes. Joe said to him, 'You rushed into that deal, didn't you? I never saw such a rushin' buyer.' Several people were passing by. The remark was overheard.

I walked away and thought no more about it. Then the rumours began to fly. 'Have you seen any Russians here? I heard there was one buying.'

'You won't get any troopers today – the Russian Buyer is after them.'

'Have you seen the Russian Buyer? He's looking for a hundred remounts for the Russian Army.'

'There's the Russian Buyer – look!' A tall pale-complexioned man in a fur hat was inspecting a horse, and at once a crowd collected. Somebody pushed forward and asked the fur-hatted one, 'Do you speak English?'

'What the hell are you raving about? Who do you think I am? The Russian Buyer?'

'Are you not from Russia then?'

'No. I'm from Mullingar.'

When rumours were flying, I often found it hard to get anyone to tell me what was going on. This was to do with being a woman in a male-dominated profession. I never met with aggression or even scorn, but I was sometimes laughed at, fairly kindly. After a time, I began to feel that I'd been accepted and there wasn't a problem – except the absence of loos at horse fairs.

The most galling thing I had to put up with was knowing that a lot of people assumed that a man must be financing me. I bought a half-spoiled filly in Limerick when I was about eighteen, and someone said, 'Whoever's paying for that one won't send you out for another.' I heard the same sort of comments when I was buying cattle.

It has been suggested to me that people in England were less sexist, but I didn't find them so. For years, the man who bought police horses from me kept up the pretence with his customers that I was a man. I discovered this when I got a letter from a police representative starting, 'Dear Mr Smithwick ...'

I told this story to an elderly Irish dealer who said, 'I've nothing against women, but it's best not to tell them anything. What they don't know won't trouble them.' Sadly enough, there are still plenty who would agree with him – although not many who would admit it.

*

It was not a good idea to stay in Ballinasloe overnight on the Sunday. Not, that is, if you wanted to sleep. Wolfe Tone discovered this two hundred years ago. We used to stay in Athlone or Banagher if we wanted to be on the move early on Monday, but before I was married I always went home.

As Monday progressed, the better-class horses thinned out and droves of Clydesdale-type youngsters began to come in from the north midlands. They ran loose and I can remember when they made a pound a leg or a fiver for a good one. Older horses' value was dictated by their weight.

Later on Monday, preparations started for the great sheep fair on the Tuesday. The horses would gradually be edged out of the way as lorry loads of sheep pens arrived and were erected. (Riders schooled their horses over these, knocking them flat and getting richly deserved abuse.) Soon after, sheep began to stream in from all sides. By mid-afternoon, all the roads leading to the green were crammed with sheep travelling on foot, while lorry drivers inched their way along, carrying yet more sheep, and other lorries tried to get away with loads of horses.

The fair offered both the best and the worst. Troopers and average working hunters – 'trading horses' – were scarce. You could see some of the best young showhorses in the country and, a few yards away, a bunch of tired, ancient donkeys changing hands.

Talking of donkeys, I remember an incident a few years ago when a farmer sold a donkey to a neighbour for £20 cash. The neighbour paid and the two went off to have a drink on the deal. Possibly two drinks. They were gone for some time, leaving the donkey tied to the fence. After a while, another buyer noticed the donkey and asked a tinker who was standing nearby, 'How much for the ass?'

'£30,' said the tinker.

After some bargaining, a price of £20 was agreed on, and buyer number two paid the tinker, also in cash. The tinker then prudently vanished and buyer number two untied the donkey and led him away. He was leaving the green when he met buyer number one, returning from the pub.

'Where are you going with the ass?'

'I just bought him off a tinker for £20. I'm taking him home.'

'You are not then. I bought him off this man here for the same money.' A noisy row developed; sides were taken, a crowd gathered. The first buyer got the donkey. The second went home, sadder, wiser and poorer.

*

There is no question but that some stallions sire progeny with a big jump in them, regardless of their own jumping ability. Once a stallion had made a name as a sire of jumpers, every young horse on offer seemed to be by him. This in pre-registration, pre-passport days.

Irish draughts were out of fashion, and many of their progeny acquired a new pedigree and a thoroughbred sire in order to make them more saleable. I tried to stick to those which were genuinely by thoroughbreds, with a preference for proven sires like Prefairy, Arctic Que or Middle Temple.

Not all my best purchases were by well-known stallions, however. Two, bought on the same afternoon, were by sires forgotten today, although one had been second in the Derby. Moidore was standing at a nominal fee at Bob Hodgin's Blackwater Stud when he sired Pimms. When John and I first saw Pimms, in January 1970, he was sheltering behind a hedge from a storm of driving sleet. He had his back up and his head down, and neither of us suspected that he was anything out of the ordinary. He was a big brown gelding, raw-boned, angular and rather coarse. He cost £165. I doubt if we would have bought him, even at that modest price, if we hadn't already bought three lucky animals from his breeder, Patrick Scanlan. He was twice to jump double clears in the Nations' Cup at Dublin for Germany, and had a distinguished jumping career. I once heard a commentator describe him as a 'typical Hannoverian'.

That wintry day when we bought Pimms, we were tempted to spend the remaining hours of daylight warming ourselves in the Scanlans' kitchen, but Patrick told us of another colt near Killaloe, owned by John Keogh. This one was by another unknown sire, the unregistered thoroughbred Scratchy. He was a lovely mover, but we felt we were pushing the boat out when we gave £200 for him. We went home, little imagining how many thousands our two colts would win between them. The Scratchy colt, named Clare Glens, won a lot of prizes for Graham Fletcher, including the Horse and Hound Cup at Wembley, before leg trouble cut his career short. He was more of a blood horse than Pimms, and both were hard to beat at their best.

*

Every horse I have ever bought has been given a name. I gave names to the horses I bred, too, but they were usually changed. Charity was sold for £450 in a bad year and looked like a handsome gift. At three, she was reserve champion in the 'Young Irelander' at Millstreet and sold for the then record price of £8600. I had no idea until afterwards that she was my horse as she was now called Philip's Delight. I called another foal Galloping Hogan, and would never have recognized him as Abbervale Dream, the world-class showjumper.

I named my dealing horses for easy reference. If one was part of a consignment of a dozen, I didn't take much trouble, often using the previous owner's surname or an allusion to an incident now long forgotten. Thus, Gilligan, Clancy, Casey and dozens more. Place-names and those deriving from the breeding are self-explanatory. Less obviously, Jane Lane was by Highland Flight and George Best could kick hard and accurately. One name brings back a train of events I haven't thought of for years – Ketchup.

Ketchup was an attractive grey mare with a temperament to match. I bought her off the land from an elderly bachelor, and pro-mised to collect her within a week. A day or two later the owner, who was called Jim, rode her into my yard. It was a bit farther than he thought, he said. Over twenty-five miles. He didn't seem tired (the mare did), although he must have been well over fifty and had ridden the four-year-old bareback all the way. He was worried about getting home to milk, though, and wouldn't wait even for a cup of tea.

Thinking how lucky it was that I'd been at home when he arrived, I drove Jim home as fast as I could. So fast indeed that, when we got there, he assured me that there was time to get both of us something to eat. I protested. He insisted. It was a cold day and I sat in the un-heated kitchen huddled in a duffel coat while Jim plugged in the kettle and put something, I couldn't see what, on the gas ring.

It turned out to be a tin of herrings in tomato sauce. The tin, not being punctured, exploded, liberally daubing the ceiling with tomato sauce, while herrings flew in all directions. One landed in the milk jug. I got a slight scald on the hand from a blob of flying sauce. I said I'd better be getting home and refused biscuits. Jim turned down my offer to help clean up the mess. At home, somehow I couldn't get away from the small of herrings in tomato sauce. It seemed to follow me about. So did the cat. I took off my duffel coat and tipped a herring or two out of the hood. I'd been lucky not to be hit in the face by one. I got out my diary and entered up the new mare as Ketchup.

CHAPTER TWENTY-FOUR

A Late Vocation

It couldn't last. Beef prices crashed and there was an acute recession in Britain. The recession hit the horse trade and I had an unpleasant interlude in hospital. We redoubled our efforts to make a living in half a dozen ways at once. At the same time, my mother, for many years a semi-invalid, became housebound and needed someone always within call.

Here I should mention Molly, who really deserves a chapter or even a book to herself. Molly Leo came as a temporary help in the house when I was about sixteen. She remained for almost fifty years, only leaving me to help my daughter, Diana, when she got married. She helped with the grandchildren, and was loved like an extra grandmother. Without Molly, I'd have found it difficult to manage when my mother was terminally ill. Diana was only eight or nine years old, John was busy on the farm and prices were sliding every day. When Molly died in 1999 she was in her mid-eighties. She never seemed to change, and all our lives are the poorer without her.

When Molly and I were fully occupied with my mother, Diana and the house, I had to do most of my horse business on the phone, as I couldn't be away at fairs and sales for whole days at a time. John and I split our responsibilities more, allowing me to go in search of horses while he concentrated on the farm. We were doing with only occasional paid help outside. Back on my own, I tried hard to avoid making any mistakes. I took my time making a bargain, in spite of the helpers who kept assuring me that 'long churning makes bad butter'. True, as it happens. Long deals are unavoidable if you have a limit you can't pass. They are unavoidable if the seller has an inflated idea of his horse's value. 'Give him, and give him lucky,' is a favourite exhortation as a deal nears its climax. I have a feeling, however absurd, that there is something in this.

The horse unwillingly given after half a day's bargaining, by someone who is certain he is being robbed, is seldom lucky in my experience. And these deals are always in the seller's favour. If the animal were really cheap, he wouldn't be hanging about all day. A horse doesn't have a value like a pound of tea. He is worth what you can get for him.

Another step I took at this difficult time was to start finding some horses on commission for private customers. I'd done this before and got caught once or twice, being obliged to buy the horse myself because the customer suddenly took fright. Now, I was older and tougher and resolved to give it another go.

One of my best private customers was the late Alma Brooke. She bought a lot of horses from me and I also bought hunt horses for the Eridge when she was joint master, on commission. On one occasion, she arrived at Crannagh, looking for a high-class broken horse. I simply hadn't time to find one, buy it and take profit, so I took her to see a dealer who had a yard full of ridden horses, good, bad and excellent.

This dealer, whom I had better call Charlie, was an artist at selling, varying his tactics according to his customer. I took a man to see him who wanted a cob for his daughter, but went away with two hunted horses, a three-year-old and two cobs. This was achieved with a sort of blarneying bonhomie. Charlie could see that my English customer was all ready to be charmed by a bit of stage Irish. This sort of thing is called paddywhackery. It worked like a charm.

Charlie was no fool. Neither was Alma, and she was Irish and impervious to paddywhackery. Charlie sized her up and then showed her a brown horse, very nice, very expensive. Alma was plainly taken by the brown, but the price asked made her pause, as well it might. She hesitated. Charlie pulled out all the stops. 'I hate to part with my little horse,' he said. 'Of all the horses I have, this one's my favourite.' He stroked its neck fondly and looked as if he might be about to cry.

'In that case,' said Alma briskly, 'I wouldn't dream of taking him away from you. I can see how much he means to you.' With that, she returned to the car and said to me, 'Poor man, I was so sorry for him.'

Charlie's comments about Alma when I met him next were not favourable – or even printable. He was a loss to the stage, but that time he overplayed his part.

*

As I drove about dealing, and spent increased time at home wishing I could be on the roads, I realized that the halcyon days, when sharp observation and quick wits could make money without recourse to dishonesty, were going fast. It had become almost impossible to find a good 'trimmer'.

A trimmer is a horse with quality and good action, whose better points are concealed by what the cosmetic advertisements call 'unwanted hair'. Things to look out for were a small head, well set on, a narrow shoulder, flat bone and free action. Given these, a horse could get away with, say, wide hips and big feet. A good trimmer was worth most untouched. Farmers whose main business was cows used to make a frightful mess with scissors and clippers in an attempt to smarten up their horses. Clipping the sides of the mane left no alternative but to hog it all off, and clipping the sides and underneath of a tail left the buyer with an insoluble problem. The clipped hair grew sideways rather than downwards and was almost impossible to pull out.

My best trimmer was called First House. I literally bought him out of the plough, an unbacked five-year-old. I rode him home barebacked and he was dog-quiet but rather clumsy. He was not, to use a favourite expression, as handy as a glove. Nor even, to use another, as handy as a flat-iron.

I have never had to trim up a horse so burdened with superfluous hair. It hung below his neck both sides, his tail brushed his fetlocks and hair clothed his legs right down to the ground. He cost £50 at a time when you could get £5 for a bag of horsehair. I got a whole bagful off First House and there was plenty to spare. Having pulled his mane, I plaited it with rubber bands to make it lie on the right side. I pulled his tail, and the hair came out in great hanks without appearing to bother him. I singed his whiskers and got down to his legs with comb and scissors. There was flat bone under all that wool. I led my frog turned prince into the stable, filled a sack with his mane and tail and swept the rest into a large heap.

I'd hardly finished when those eminent dealers Nat Galway-Greer and Willie McCaldin drove into the yard. I pulled my horse out again and sold him in minutes for my asking price of £80. If I'd had time to look my handiwork more carefully, I'd have asked much more. First House changed hands soon afterwards for £300, and within six weeks was reserve champion heavyweight at the Dublin Horse Show.

Horses with broad crests to their necks are difficult to plait. I bought a grey mare in Wexford with a noticeably broad crest, and I remember thinking they'd made a good job of plaiting her up. However, the crafty owner had clipped a strip down the centre of her neck, leaving part of the mane on each side. He then plaited what was left most artfully. When the plaits were out, the mane fell either side of her neck, while the central swathe was already starting to grow like a hedge. There was nothing for it but to clip the lot.

*

John didn't like me going on buying trips in the nearby mountains without him because of my habit of getting lost. He got lost himself, all the time, but that just made him worry more about me. Even in the late seventies, farming was a poor job in the Slieve Felim mountains. Incomes were boosted by the brewing of poteen rather than subsidies; signposts were scarce.

Before the roads were tarred, you could follow a reasonably good boreen which would gradually narrow and eventually disappear altogether. You were lucky if there was anywhere to turn. Some of the people who lived in great poverty in this area were among the most charming and hospitable I have ever met. Their lives were hard; few had piped water or electricity. None had telephones.

Many young couples had bought electric devices but were still waiting for the power to come. One newly married pair got a washing-machine but were away for the day when the power was finally switched on. Only the old mother was there. She filled the washing-machine with cream and, by the time the couple returned, she had made the butter.

Some yards where there was no motor car were approached by cart tracks. One day, John and I were sitting in the car debating whether to risk turning up a track which was crossed by a broad stream (not a flood – a fixture). After a time, a boy rode past on a bike and I asked him if I could drive through the water without getting stuck. 'You can,' he said, 'John Kennedy drove his car through there an hour ago.'

We were in the exact centre of the stream when the engine spluttered and died. And that was where John Kennedy found us when he returned with his car some time later. The boy hadn't mentioned that it was of the horse-drawn variety.

Not far away, in a remote spot, lived a man with his father and uncle, both of whom were old and suffered from 'old pains'. They spent most of the winter in bed. When I bought a horse from the son, I had to go and talk to father and uncle before the deal could be completed. They were in a big brass bed, propped against the pillows sitting side by side. They wore coats, waistcoats, flannel shirts and hats. This was less eccentric than it sounds, as the house was cold and draughty. They didn't get on too well and squabbled incessantly over their hearing-aid. Neither would let the other use it; both needed it. The conversation was one-sided. Afterwards, one of them wrote me a let-ter in the sort of beautiful copperplate you find on Victorian deeds.

Dogs ran loose on every farm. They came to meet you if there was nobody at home, and most were the sort of dog you don't argue with. At one farm, the dog must have been asleep and didn't hear me when I arrived. The door was open, so I knocked and shouted, 'Anybody at home?' There was. A dog as big as a calf and it bit me. The farmer appeared. 'Your dog's bitten me,' I told him.

'Ah. Has he? He's playful. I hope he didn't bite through your wellington.'

'No, he's bitten my hand,' I said, examining it. The dog looked as if he was considering a second helping, and I retreated to the car in a hurry.

'You're all right so,' said the farmer. 'A hand will mend, but wellingtons is dear to buy.' I insisted he tie up his dog before I got out of the car again – he had a good horse to sell. 'You haven't a pile of courage,' he said scornfully as he led it away. This annoyed me, and my hand was swelling, so I left his horse.

Some five years later, I got a letter which appeared to be in code. No address, no signature. It was short and to the point.

Miss. The dog is dead. Come back.

Completely bewildered, I put it away, and it was another six months later when I met the ex-dog owner at Thurles fair. 'Didn't you get my letter?' he demanded. He was selling a younger horse and I bought it. In the street, it was standing on level ground. This isn't as irrelevant as it might seem. In the mountains, where I bought so many colts, there could be a difference of three inches in the height of one side of a horse and the other. If he was facing directly uphill, he measured more than his height; if downhill, less. Of course, a too small horse was certain to grow – according to the man selling him. 'His brother was smaller than that at three and he grew till he was six.'

'He was a July foal.' A favourite excuse. 'Everything by that sire (out of that mare) grows to 16.2.' 'His mother hadn't any milk.' 'He'll look bigger when he's shod/saddled/trained/on level ground.'

In my experience, small horses stay small, big horses grow. I was badly caught out by a horse which grew three inches at grass in three months. I sold him over the phone without catching him for £600. I should have asked £800.

We bought a brother of that horse from a man who took us to an out farm to see it. He asked to have the car-heater turned up because he'd lent his topcoat to a neighbour who was going courting. 'You couldn't go courting without a topcoat, could you?'

We bought the horse and, when we returned our companion to his house, the topcoat was hanging on the gate.

*

I remembered these things and many others as I sat sulkily at home, trying to augment our living. I rediscovered a minor artistic talent and put it to use painting souvenirs. I did quite well for a time. Then I began to get orders for a couple of hundred hand-painted mugs at a go, and a mildly profitable hobby became a demanding chore. Soon I was suffering from eye-strain and terminal boredom. Machine knitting and weaving were little better.

The only thing which paid while also giving me pleasure was the breeding of Border Collies. We were putting together a kennel of useful dogs which combined good temperaments with ability, and puppies sold like hot cakes. John and I went to sheepdog trials most Sundays and spent our time deep in conversation with kindred spirits.

My fondness for Border Collies and attending trials was not comparable with my feelings about horses. My greatest pleasure has always been in buying and selling them; particularly buying them. At a horse fair I always felt in my element – although I would never dream of going to a fair if I had no business there. I have bought dozens of horses at auction, but I would do that as a matter of course as I would buy sheep or cattle for the farm. A horse fair fills me with the same kind of elation as an antique sale. A dangerous emotion if not curbed.

The farming recession hit us hard, and there was a time when my puppies, added to John's working dogs, were making almost as much as the reduced horse operation.

There are two approaches to selling puppies. One is the 'I don't care as long as they pay' school, reminiscent of the dealer who said, 'If a customer comes back for a second horse, I know I didn't charge enough for the first one.' The other viewpoint is that nobody else in Ireland could possibly appreciate and look after your puppy. It is sure to be ill-treated, starved, neglected – how can you be such a monster as to part with it? Like most breeders of pedigree stock, I learned to part with my favourites philosophically. Soon, I had so much demand for puppies that I could discourage anybody who seemed unlikely to appreciate one.

One thing which became tedious was answering all the questions which each buyer in turn asked. The same questions over and over again – what does he eat? When does he get his jabs? When do we start to train him? So I wrote out an 800-word guide, entitled 'Looking after your sheepdog puppy.' This I proposed to have photo-copied, so that I could hand one over with every pup.

I can remember writing the two pages of foolscap in careful script with plenty of red underlining, and being pleased with the effect. Like other watersheds in my life, it went unrecognized at the time. I was fifty-one years old and not planning on a new career. John vetted my work and said, 'Why don't you offer it to *The Farmers' Journal* as an article?'

Fools rush in. I went straight to the telephone, asked for the editor and gave him an outline of what I'd written. When I put the phone down ten minutes later, I'd been commissioned to write a series of six articles entitled 'The Farm Dog' at £25 apiece. This stretched to ten articles and £30, and almost before I knew it I was a freelance journal-ist, writing for the main Irish farming magazines on a variety of dog- and sheep-related subjects. A year later I had my first article accepted by *The Irish Field*, extending my repertoire to horses. I wrote for the *Field* for many years.

*

My mother died in 1979. She had brought me up on tales of my literary forbears. Edith Somerville was my grandmother's first cousin and they used to share their holidays as girls. Then there was Henry Seton Merriman (a *nom-de-plume*), a wildly fashionable novelist of the early part of the century, now hopelessly dated. Other relatives included the naturalist and writer Ernest Thomson Seton and his daughter, novelist Anya Seton. More recently, my aunt, Evelyn Brodhurst-Hill, had written two successful books of memoirs and had had many political articles published in *The Spectator*. I found these facts daunting rather than encouraging. When I'd said as a girl that I'd like to be a writer, all these people were held up as examples of what I could do if I tried. I didn't try.

I began to feel that in some obscure way I owed it to my mother to have a go at least. She herself had often offered her work to publishers, but with no success.

I slunk into writing through the back door. After the first batch of articles, I tried to brighten up a (then) rather solemn magazine called *Working Sheepdog News* with a story called 'Shep at the Sheepdog Trial'. Greatly to my surprise, this resulted in a spate of letters demanding 'more about Irish Shep'. This work was unpaid at the time, but it was great fun, and I soon wrote about twenty episodes. What started as separate funny pieces gradually became a narrative. I discovered I was writing a book.

Meanwhile, I'd got the original twelve sheepdog articles printed and bound by a firm which dealt mainly with posters and dance tickets. To my utter astonishment, I sold a thousand copies and had to print more. It sold two thousand copies all told.

Author Charles Chenevix Trench, a friend of ours, then did me a good turn by sending my 'Shep' stories to his agent, David Fletcher in Edinburgh. It is well known that you can't get an agent unless you have been published, and you can't get published unless you have an agent. David sent the manuscript, entitled 'One Dog and His Man', to eight publishers, and they all returned it except for two firms which lost it between them, each blaming the other. David then advised me to consider some other occupation, but I'd had some 'glowing rejections' and asked him to try once more. The ninth firm was the Blackstaff Press, which accepted it. It appeared in 1984 and had the best notices I've ever received. Phrases like 'a little gem', 'a small masterpiece' and many more littered the reviews. It has been in print in various forms and with various publishers ever since and has even been translated into Japanese.

Pelham Books then commissioned a large handsome hardback about Border Collies, stuffed with photographs. I was in seventh heaven. A writer. Good God! Me! Well, there it was, and now I could write a novel and it would be published and I would be fêted and fussed over … rich … famous …

Long before my feet had returned to the ground, I had a letter from Collins, commissioning a novel. This threw me into a tremendous tizzy but obviously it wasn't an offer I could refuse. John had given me a course with the Writing School as a present, and I'd found it helpful in writing articles, although I don't think I learned much about novel writing from it. However, my tutor had constantly encouraged me to try a novel, so I wrote to him for help. Help which enabled me to face the task of writing a 90,000-word book, when my 'Shep' books were only a third of that length. I received the support I needed – as much confidence boosting as actual tuition – and set to work. The book, *Corporal Jack*, was, you've guessed it, about a dog.

The whole of the writing of this book was overshadowed by John's illness and death in the spring of 1985. Sometimes I wonder how it was possible to write at all – more often I wonder how I could have got through those months without something demanding to do which had to be completed on time. It isn't a time I want to dwell on. I finished the book, physically and emotionally exhausted, and although it did well, I can never think about it without remembering the circumstances of its composition.

The dog, Jack, was central to the plot, but I resisted writing a straight 'doggy' novel; especially so as the book was set in the mud and blood of the First World War, and I felt that a dog hero somehow belittled the human characters. I managed to make the dog into the lynchpin which held the story together while retaining separate plots concerning a large cast of characters. The book was a success.

I was ready to embark on something totally different, but my idea for a new novel was rejected because there wasn't a dog in it. I was asked for a speedy rethink if Collins was to commission it. I rethought, and the resulting book, *No Harp Like My Own*, did well, being my biggest financial success to date. I had had to contrive somewhat to introduce a dog and make it important without losing my basic idea, but thought I had done so without loss of integrity.

Apparently not. Around then, I went to a launch where I met a poet who told me that my work wouldn't be worth reading if I bent in any way to the will of publishers and editors. I told him what I'd done and he said gloomily, 'I suppose you know you've prostituted your soul.' Ah well.

After this, I managed to get away from the doggy label. I have stood fast in my refusal to write about dogs all the time, and have got by. Every branch of writing has its own pitfalls, and those which await the animal writer are deeper and nastier than most. I have learned to be wary of the sort of blurb which begins, 'This is the story of a man, a woman and a dog,' or 'This heart-warming tale will delight animal lovers everywhere.'

Reviewers seem to feel it their duty to belittle novels which feature animals, with patronizing allusions to Lassie and Black Beauty. And without reviews, the modern writer withers and dies. Sometimes people say that writing about animals is easier than writing about humans. It may be, but it carries the temptation to indulge in gooey sentiment. It's funny – sentiment is an emotion unknown to animals and small children, yet stories about both are often saccharine sweet.

I avoided writing another doggy book the next time, but only by substituting horses. André Deutsch published my first book of memoirs, and were also the first to accept from me a novel with no animal interest. Children's books followed. Now my illusions about wealth have faded. To succeed financially, I really believe you must find a niche and firmly stay in it, resisting all temptations to experiment. Now that I am established, with twelve published books to my name, and am also a professional editor and a holder of writers' workshops and so on, I lead a life as different as one could imagine from my old one. I still work at various jobs for my bread and butter, while my writing provides the jam.

*

This has been a hard book to write because I have tried to deal with the different lives I've led, as horse-dealer, farmer, dog-breeder and writer. If I have included little about my husband and daughter, it is only because that would have been John's wish and is Diana's. My various interests have overlapped; many doors have opened and closed for me. Nowadays, I help Diana with her antique business – which gives me the chance to go back to dealing, and saves me from taking root. I also manage three charity shops in aid of the blind, so I am kept busy and happy.

I am an optimistic and resilient person, and have needed to be when making my living in notoriously risky ways; however, writing is something you can do as long as you stay alive and retain your sanity. I love it and the spin-offs that come with it. Through writing I got to know some wonderful people whom I would otherwise never have met, and my horizons have widened. I began to live again after a bad patch.

There is so much more I might have included. Little things, buried in memory, come back unbidden. A Valentine, a thing of hearts and roses with a paper frill and of course unsigned. I knew who had sent it, which was as well. As the sender was about to post it he remembered something, and scribbled on the envelope, 'I could do with a decent three-year-old gelding, not too dear.'

But I mustn't start digging in my ragbag of a mind again, or this book will never be finished. I will just mention that the dogs are a continuing interest and enable me to look after my sheep, for you need to be more than alive and reasonably sane if you are to farm. Since starting to write this, I have moved out of my old home, just keeping the land. I have willing helpers there in Diana and her husband, Dan. Then there are those three young people without whose help this book would have been finished in half the time; my grandson Jack, born on Christmas day in the morning, and his brother and sister, Luke and Robyn. They live at Crannagh now, a lovely place to grow up in.

Time to call a halt to these reminiscences. Time to do what still gives me immense and childish pleasure. To write in neat capitals:

THE END

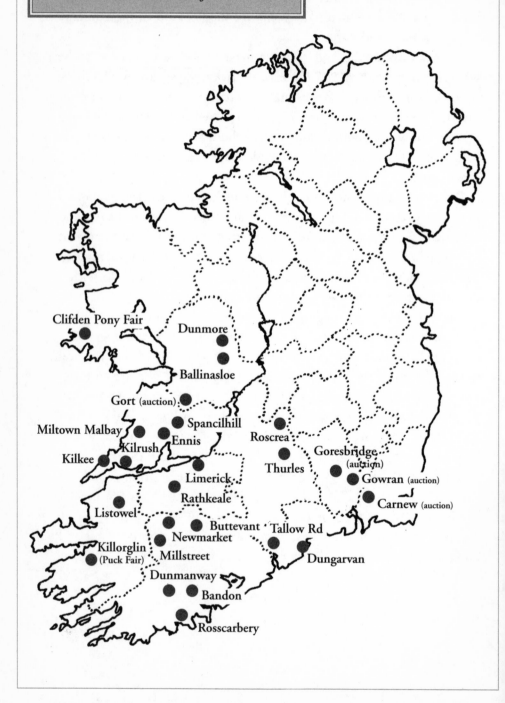

Names and Locations of Horse Fairs

Clifden Pony Fair
Dunmore
Ballinasloe
Gort (auction)
Spancilhill
Miltown Malbay
Kilrush
Ennis
Roscrea
Goresbridge (auction)
Kilkee
Thurles
Gowran (auction)
Limerick
Rathkeale
Carnew (auction)
Listowel
Buttevant
Tallow Rd
Killorglin (Puck Fair)
Newmarket
Millstreet
Dungarvan
Dunmanway
Bandon
Rosscarbery